Fondue Cookbook

Hamlyn's Fondue Cookbook

Jill Spencer

CHANCELLOR
PRESS

Acknowledgements
The author and publisher would like to thank the following for
their co-operation in supplying photographs for this book:

Argentine Beef Bureau: page 79
British Sugar Bureau: page 31
H.P. Bulmer Limited (Cider Makers), Hereford: pages 23 and 86–87
Charbonnier Table Wines: pages 62–63
Colman's Mustard: page 95
Corning Limited ('Pyroflam' shallow cook pan – orange decoration): page 83
Dutch Dairy Bureau: page 26
Farmhouse English Cheeses: page 10
Fruit Producers Council: page 106
Gale's Honey: pages 110–111
H.J. Heinz Company Limited: pages 74–75
Mazola Pure Corn Oil: pages 34 and 42
Milk Marketing Board: page 66
Russell Hobbs Limited: page 70
Sharwoods Foods Limited: page 39
Sunbeam Electric Limited (Multi-Cooker): pages 91 (using de luxe model) and 98
Swiss Cheese Union: page 19

Dexam International Limited, Haslemere, for the loan of their Spring fondue
equipment

Line drawings by Ann Rees

First published in 1989

Reprinted 1996

This edition published in 1994
by Chancellor Press an imprint of
Reed Consumer Books Ltd
Michelin House,
81 Fulham Road,
London SW3 6RB
and Auckland, Melbourne, Singapore & Toronto

ISBN 1 85152 774 5

Produced by Mandarin Offset
Printed and bound in Hong Kong

Contents

Introduction

The fondue originated in Switzerland, where it became the Swiss people's national dish. There are many legends about the fondue's origin; one story tells of the villagers who, when their food became scarce during the long cold winters, had to turn to their home-produced foods. These were, of course, cheese, wine and home-made bread. As the cheese became old and hard, the villagers used to put it in a pot with wine to soften and melt it. Hence the French word 'fondre' which, interpreted, means 'to melt'.

With more and more people going to Austria and Switzerland for their holidays, our eating habits are becoming more cosmopolitan. During the last few years, many fondue pots have been imported so that even in our shops there are a great variety to choose from. All are very attractive, whether they are made from earthenware, stainless steel, copper, coloured or patterned enamel.

A fondue, whether cheese, bourguignonne or the more unusual sweet, is a super way to entertain as it is great fun, makes little work for the hostess and creates an informal relaxed evening. Guests can enjoy participating, and the selection of food items which can be used as 'dippers' adds enormous variety and interest.

Some more exciting ideas for entertaining are given in the tabletop section in this book. Tabletop cookery includes both savoury and sweet recipes which, for entertaining purposes, can be cooked actually at the table in front of your guests. It is always rather fun, and impressive too, to try tabletop cookery yourself, instead of watching the waiter in your favourite restaurant performing this.

At the end of the book, there are menu suggestions and drinks recipes – all combining to make your fondue or tabletop party a success.

Metrication and safety hints

Notes on metrication

In this book quantities have been given in metric, Imperial and American measures. Exact conversion from Imperial to metric measures does not usually give very convenient working quantities and so for greater convenience we have rounded off metric measures into units of 25 grammes. The table below shows recommended equivalents.

Ounces/fluid ounces	Approx. g and ml to nearest whole figure	Recommended conversion to nearest unit of 25
1	28	25
2	57	50
3	85	75
4	113	100
5 ($\frac{1}{4}$ pint)	142	150
6	170	175
7	198	200
8 ($\frac{1}{2}$ lb)	226	225
9	255	250
10 ($\frac{1}{2}$ pint)	283	275
11	311	300
12	340	350
13	368	375
14	397	400
15 ($\frac{3}{4}$ pint)	425	425
16 (1 lb)	454	450
17	482	475
18	510	500
19	539	550
20 (1 pint)	567	575

NOTE: When converting quantities over 20 oz, first add the appropriate figures in the centre column, then adjust to the nearest unit of 25. As a general guide, 1 kg (1000 g) equals 2·2 lb or about 2 lb 3 oz; 1 litre (1000 ml) equals 1·76 pints or almost exactly 1$\frac{3}{4}$ pints.

Liquid measures The millilitre is a very small unit of measurement and we felt that to use decilitres (units of 100 ml) would be less cumbersome. In most cases it is perfectly satisfactory to round off the exact millilitre conversion to the nearest decilitre, except for $\frac{1}{4}$ pint; thus $\frac{1}{4}$ pint (142 ml) is 1·5 dl, $\frac{1}{2}$ pint (283 ml) is 3 dl, $\frac{3}{4}$ pint (425 ml) is 4·5 dl, and 1 pint (567 ml) is 6 dl. For quantities over 1 pint we have used litres and fractions of a litre.

Can sizes Because at present cans are marked with the exact (usually to the nearest whole number) metric equivalent of the Imperial weight of the contents, we have followed this practice when giving can sizes. Thus the equivalent of a 14-oz can of tomatoes would be a 397-g can.

Tablespoons You will note that sometimes measurements are given in tablespoons; the spoon used is the British Standard measuring spoon of 17·7 millilitres.

All spoon measures are level unless indicated otherwise.

Notes for American users

Each recipe in this book has an American column giving U.S. cup measures for the ingredients. The following list gives American equivalents or substitutes for some terms used in the book.

BRITISH	AMERICAN
Baking tin	Baking pan
Cocktail stick	Wooden toothpick
Frying pan	Skillet
Greaseproof paper	Wax paper
Grill	Broil/broiler
Kitchen paper	Paper towels
Mixer/liquidiser	Mixer/blender
Piping bag	Pastry bag
Piping tube	Nozzle/tip
Stoned	Pitted
Whisk	Whip/beat

NOTE: The British pint measures 20 fluid ounces whereas the American pint equals 16 fluid ounces.

Notes for Australian users

Quantities in the recipes in this book are given in metric, Imperial and American measures. The old Australian standard measuring cup is the same as the American standard 8-fluid ounce cup; the new Australian cup is bigger and holds 250 ml. Note also that the Australian standard tablespoon holds 20 ml and is therefore bigger than either the American (14·2 ml) or the Imperial (17·7 ml). The table below gives a comparison.

AMERICAN	BRITISH	AUSTRALIAN
1 teaspoon	1 teaspoon	1 teaspoon
1 tablespoon	1 tablespoon	1 tablespoon
3 tablespoons	2 tablespoons	2 tablespoons
4 tablespoons	3$\frac{1}{2}$ tablespoons	3 tablespoons
5 tablespoons	4 tablespoons	3$\frac{1}{2}$ tablespoons

Safety hints

Do not overfill the fondue pan with oil when serving a fondue bourguignonne; never fill more than two-thirds full.

Take care not to overheat the oil. It is a good idea initially to heat the oil on the top of the cooker until it reaches approximately 360°F (182°C) or if you have no thermometer, drop a small piece of bread in the oil. If it browns in under a minute, the oil is at the correct temperature.

Do not put too much food in the oil at any one time, as this will cause the oil to froth up and possibly overflow. It will also reduce the temperature of the oil rather rapidly.

Do not eat meat straight from the fondue fork as it gets very hot and can burn the mouth.

Always make sure that the burner is secure on the table and that the handle of the fondue pan cannot be knocked.

Make sure the table is well protected with mats under the burner, as this tends to get very hot and could mark the tabletop.

When flambéing a dish do not bend right over it, stand well back in case your hair gets singed!

Cheese Fondues

One usually associates the word fondue with cheese, although there are many variations as you will see further on in the book. There is a great number of cheese fondues, varying from the traditional one using Swiss cheeses to fondues using different cheeses and with other ingredients added to the fondue pot as well!

In Switzerland it is traditional to serve a glass of kirsch during the meal, but a glass of the wine used in the fondue is equally acceptable. An old Swiss custom which can be great fun at parties is that whoever drops a cube of bread into the fondue must carry out a forfeit. If it is a woman, she must kiss every man present, or if it is a man, he is more unlucky – he has to buy a bottle of wine for each of the guests! If anyone should lose their bread a second time, then they have to give the next fondue party!

The selection of 'dippers' or 'dunkers' is endless – cubes of French bread, curried bread cubes (fried in butter with a little curry powder), toasted brown bread cubes, raw vegetables, cooked meats, shellfish and many others.

Here are a few hints that may help you when serving a cheese fondue:

a)   Always use a dry wine in a fondue; to make the wine drier add a few drops of lemon juice.

b)   If the fondue should curdle, a little lemon juice will rectify this problem.

c)   If too thin, stir in a little more cheese, or cornflour blended with a little wine.

d)   If the fondue becomes too thick, stir in some warm wine.

e)   Remember, cheese burns easily, so it is best to use a thick-based pot, preferably flameproof pottery. The flame should always be kept low and constant stirring is necessary until the cheese has melted and thickened.

Suitable wines to use in a cheese fondue and to serve with it are chablis, hock, riesling or any other dry white wine.

Farmhouse fondue

IMPERIAL/METRIC	AMERICAN
1 clove garlic	1 clove garlic
1 lb/450 g Cheddar cheese, grated	4 cups grated Cheddar cheese
¼ pint/1·5 dl milk	⅔ cup milk
salt and pepper	salt and pepper
pinch dry mustard	pinch dry mustard
pinch nutmeg	pinch nutmeg
2 tablespoons dry white wine (optional)	3 tablespoons dry white wine (optional)

Rub the inside of a fondue pan with the cut clove of garlic. Add the cheese and melt over a gentle heat, stirring continuously. Stir in the remaining ingredients. Cook until thickened and creamy, stirring all the time.

TO SERVE: Use cubes of fried bread, pretzels and bread sticks to dip into the fondue.

NOTE: This is not a stringy fondue.

Serves 4

Illustrated on page 10

Caraway fondue

IMPERIAL/METRIC	AMERICAN
1 clove garlic	1 clove garlic
¾ pint/4·5 dl dry white wine	2 cups dry white wine
1 lb/450 g Emmenthal cheese, grated	4 cups grated Emmenthal cheese
2 tablespoons flour	3 tablespoons all-purpose flour
1 tablespoon caraway seeds	1 tablespoon caraway seeds
freshly ground black pepper	freshly ground black pepper
2 tablespoons chopped parsley	3 tablespoons chopped parsley

Rub the inside of a fondue pan with the cut clove of garlic. Pour in the wine and heat gently. Gradually stir in the cheese and flour, mixed. When the cheese has melted, stir in the caraway seeds, pepper and parsley.

TO SERVE: Use cubes of rye bread for dipping.

Serves 4

Spinach fondue

IMPERIAL/METRIC	AMERICAN
1 pint/6 dl dry white wine	2½ cups dry white wine
1 lb/450 g Swiss cheese, grated	4 cups grated Swiss cheese
2 tablespoons cornflour	3 tablespoons cornstarch
4 tablespoons kirsch	⅓ cup kirsch
1 (8-oz/227-g) packet frozen spinach	1 (8-oz) package frozen spinach
pinch nutmeg	pinch nutmeg
pinch salt	pinch salt
freshly ground black pepper	freshly ground black pepper

Pour the wine into a fondue pan and heat gently. Add the cheese and cornflour gradually and allow the cheese to melt, stirring continuously. Add the kirsch.

Cook the spinach according to the instructions on the packet and drain well. Add the spinach to the fondue with the nutmeg, salt and black pepper. Reheat and serve.

TO SERVE: Use small frankfurters or sausages for dipping.

Serves 4

Crab fondue

IMPERIAL/METRIC	AMERICAN
1 clove garlic	1 clove garlic
1 pint/6 dl white wine	2½ cups white wine
1 lb/450 g Gruyère cheese, grated	4 cups grated Gruyère cheese
2 tablespoons cornflour	3 tablespoons cornstarch
1 (8-oz/227-g) can crab meat	1 (8-oz) can crab meat
freshly ground black pepper	freshly ground black pepper
paprika pepper	paprika pepper

Rub the inside of a fondue pan with the cut clove of garlic. Pour in the white wine and heat gently. Gradually stir in the cheese and cornflour, mixed, and allow the cheese to melt. Add the crab meat and pepper, and reheat until thick, stirring. Sprinkle with paprika pepper.

TO SERVE: Use cubes of fried bread.

Serves 4

3-cheese fondue

IMPERIAL/METRIC	AMERICAN
1 clove garlic	1 clove garlic
2 oz/50 g butter	¼ cup butter
1-2 sticks celery, finely chopped	1-2 stalks celery, finely chopped
½ pint/3 dl dry white wine	1¼ cups dry white wine
12 oz/350 g Emmenthal cheese, grated	3 cups grated Emmenthal cheese
12 oz/350 g Gruyère cheese, grated	3 cups grated Gruyère cheese
2 oz/50 g Parmesan cheese, grated	½ cup grated Parmesan cheese
pinch dry mustard	pinch dry mustard
pinch nutmeg	pinch nutmeg
pinch cayenne pepper	pinch cayenne pepper
3 teaspoons cornflour	3 teaspoons cornstarch
2 tablespoons brandy	3 tablespoons brandy

Rub the inside of a fondue pan with the cut clove of garlic. Add the butter and allow to melt. Fry the celery for 5-10 minutes. Stir in the wine and heat gently. Gradually add the cheeses, stirring until melted. Season with the mustard, nutmeg and cayenne pepper. Blend the cornflour with the brandy and add to the fondue. Bring to the boil and cook for 10 minutes, stirring all the time.

TO SERVE: Use peeled shrimps and bite-sized pieces of brown or French bread to dip into the fondue.

Serves 4

Illustrated opposite

Danish Samsoe fondue

IMPERIAL/METRIC	AMERICAN
1 pint/6 dl beer	2½ cups beer
1 lb/450 g Samsoe cheese, grated	4 cups grated Samsoe cheese
2 tablespoons flour	3 tablespoons all-purpose flour
4 tablespoons dry white wine	⅓ cup dry white wine
3 tablespoons chopped parsley	4 tablespoons chopped parsley

Heat the beer in a fondue pan and add the cheese and flour, mixed, gradually. Stir continuously until the cheese has melted. Stir in the wine and parsley then reheat and serve.

TO SERVE: Use cubes of French bread to dip.

Serves 4

Far Eastern fondue

IMPERIAL/METRIC	AMERICAN
1 clove garlic	1 clove garlic
½ pint/3 dl dry white wine	1¼ cups dry white wine
1 lb/450 g Swiss cheese, grated	4 cups grated Swiss cheese
8 oz/225 g Emmenthal cheese, grated	2 cups grated Emmenthal cheese
2 teaspoons cornflour	2 teaspoons cornstarch
1-2 tablespoons curry powder	2-3 tablespoons curry powder
1 tablespoon brandy	1 tablespoon brandy
pinch salt	pinch salt
1 teaspoon lemon juice	1 teaspoon lemon juice
freshly ground black pepper	freshly ground black pepper

Rub the inside of the fondue pan with the cut clove of garlic. Pour in the wine and heat gently. Gradually add the cheeses, stirring all the time. Combine the cornflour, curry powder and brandy, and stir into the fondue. Continue stirring until the fondue is thick. Add the salt, lemon juice and black pepper to taste.

TO SERVE: Use pumpernickel bread and sticks of celery to dip into the fondue.

Serves 4-6

Horseradish fondue

IMPERIAL/METRIC	AMERICAN
½ oz/15 g butter	1 tablespoon butter
8 oz/225 g Cheddar cheese, grated	2 cups grated Cheddar cheese
4 tablespoons milk	⅓ cup milk
1 tablespoon Worcestershire sauce	1 tablespoon Worcestershire sauce
2 teaspoons dried grated horseradish	2 teaspoons dried grated horseradish
salt and pepper	salt and pepper
1 tablespoon flour	1 tablespoon all-purpose flour
1 tablespoon water	1 tablespoon water
1 tablespoon dry white wine	1 tablespoon dry white wine

Place the butter and cheese together in a fondue pan and allow to melt. Stir in the milk, Worcestershire sauce, horseradish and seasoning. Blend the flour with the water and stir into the fondue. When smooth and thick add the white wine and reheat, stirring.

TO SERVE: Use artichoke hearts, cubes of ham and florets of cauliflower.

Serves 2

Gorgonzola fondue

IMPERIAL/METRIC	AMERICAN
8 oz/225 g Gorgonzola cheese, grated or crumbled	2 cups grated or crumbled Gorgonzola or other blue cheese
8 oz/225 g Gruyère cheese, grated	2 cups grated Gruyère cheese
2 tablespoons flour	3 tablespoons all-purpose flour
8 fl oz/2·5 dl dry white wine	1 cup dry white wine
1 clove garlic, crushed	1 clove garlic, crushed
4 tablespoons kirsch	$\frac{1}{3}$ cup kirsch
pinch nutmeg	pinch nutmeg
freshly ground black pepper	freshly ground black pepper

Mix the cheeses with the flour. Heat the wine and garlic in a fondue pan. Add the cheese gradually, stirring continuously and allowing each amount to melt before adding more. When all the cheese has been added and the mixture is smooth, stir in the kirsch, nutmeg and pepper to taste.
TO SERVE: Use cubes of toasted bread.

Serves 4

Mussel fondue

IMPERIAL/METRIC	AMERICAN
1 clove garlic	1 clove garlic
$\frac{1}{4}$ pint/1·5 dl dry white wine	$\frac{2}{3}$ cup dry white wine
1 lb/450 g Emmenthal cheese, grated	4 cups grated Emmenthal cheese
1 tablespoon cornflour	1 tablespoon cornstarch
1 tablespoon chopped parsley	1 tablespoon chopped parsley
salt and pepper	salt and pepper
1 tablespoon dry sherry	1 tablespoon dry sherry
1 (6-oz/170-g) jar smoked mussels, chopped	1 (6-oz) jar smoked mussels, chopped

Rub the inside of a fondue pan with the cut clove of garlic. Pour the wine into the pan and heat gently. Gradually add the cheese and cornflour, mixed, stirring continuously until all the cheese has melted. Stir in the remaining ingredients and heat until thickened.
TO SERVE: Use cubes of French bread to dip into the fondue.

Serves 4

Traditional cheese fondue (Neuchâtel fondue)

IMPERIAL/METRIC	AMERICAN
1 clove garlic	1 clove garlic
¼ pint/1·5 dl dry white wine	⅔ cup dry white wine
1 teaspoon lemon juice	1 teaspoon lemon juice
10 oz/275 g Emmenthal cheese, grated	2½ cups grated Emmenthal cheese
10 oz/275 g Gruyère cheese, grated	2½ cups grated Gruyère cheese
1 tablespoon cornflour	1 tablespoon cornstarch
3 tablespoons kirsch	4 tablespoons kirsch
pinch white pepper	pinch white pepper
pinch ground nutmeg	pinch ground nutmeg
pinch paprika pepper	pinch paprika pepper

Rub the inside of a fondue pan with the cut clove of garlic. Pour the wine into the pan with the lemon juice and heat gently. Gradually add the cheese, stirring in a 'figure of eight' motion, until all the cheese is combined.

When the mixture begins to bubble, blend the cornflour and kirsch together and add to the fondue. Continue to cook gently for a further 2-3 minutes and season, according to taste, with the pepper, nutmeg and paprika.

TO SERVE: Use cubes of French bread.

Serves 4

Illustrated opposite

Parmesan fondue

IMPERIAL/METRIC	AMERICAN
3 eggs	3 eggs
4 oz/100 g Parmesan cheese, grated	1 cup grated Parmesan cheese
2 oz/50 g unsalted butter	¼ cup sweet butter
salt and pepper	salt and pepper

Whisk the eggs until frothy. Gradually add the remaining ingredients. Pour into a fondue pan and heat gently, stirring all the time, until the mixture resembles thick cream. *Take care not to overcook.* Serve at once.

TO SERVE: Cut pieces of celery and French bread to dip.

NOTE: This is not a stringy fondue.

Serves 2

Clover fondue

IMPERIAL/METRIC	AMERICAN
1 clove garlic	1 clove garlic
¾ pint/4·5 dl dry white wine	2 cups dry white wine
1 lb/450 g Emmenthal cheese, grated	4 cups grated Emmenthal cheese
2 oz/50 g Sapsago cheese, grated (see note)	½ cup grated Sapsago cheese (see note)
1 oz/25 g flour	¼ cup all-purpose flour
4 tablespoons kirsch	⅓ cup kirsch
pinch nutmeg	pinch nutmeg
freshly ground black pepper	freshly ground black pepper

Rub the inside of a fondue pan with the cut clove of garlic. Pour in the wine and heat gently. Gradually add the cheeses and flour, mixed, stirring continuously until all the cheese has melted. When the mixture is smooth and thick, stir in the remaining ingredients.

TO SERVE: Use sticks of celery and pieces of carrot.

NOTE: Sapsago cheese is a Swiss hard, dried cheese flavoured with powdered clover leaves. Derby sage cheese may be substituted.

Serves 4

Baghdad fondue

IMPERIAL/METRIC	AMERICAN
1 clove garlic	1 clove garlic
¾ pint/4·5 dl white wine	2 cups white wine
1 lb/450 g Gruyère cheese, grated	4 cups grated Gruyère cheese
8 oz/225 g Emmenthal cheese, grated	2 cups grated Emmenthal cheese
1 tablespoon cornflour	1 tablespoon cornstarch
2 tablespoons curry powder	3 tablespoons curry powder
2 tablespoons dry sherry	3 tablespoons dry sherry
grated rind of ½ lemon	grated rind of ½ lemon
freshly ground black pepper	freshly ground black pepper

Rub the inside of a fondue pan with the cut clove of garlic. Pour in the wine and heat gently. Gradually add the cheeses, stirring constantly until melted.

Combine the cornflour and curry powder and blend with the sherry. Add to the cheese mixture and cook until thickened. Stir in the lemon rind and black pepper.

TO SERVE: Frankfurter sausages make a pleasant change from bread to dip.

Serves 4-6

Anchovy fondue

IMPERIAL/METRIC	AMERICAN
1 oz/25 g butter	2 tablespoons butter
1 lb/450 g Cheddar cheese, grated	4 cups grated Cheddar cheese
1½ tablespoons cornflour	2 tablespoons cornstarch
¼ pint/1·5 dl warmed milk	⅔ cup warmed milk
1 tablespoon anchovy essence	1 tablespoon anchovy extract
salt and pepper	salt and pepper
few drops Tabasco sauce	few drops Tabasco sauce
2 eggs, separated	2 eggs, separated
2 tablespoons dry sherry	3 tablespoons dry sherry

Place the butter and cheese in a fondue pan and stir over a gentle heat until the cheese has melted. Combine the cornflour, warmed milk, anchovy essence, salt, pepper and Tabasco sauce and stir into the melted cheese. Cook until the mixture thickens, stirring all the time.

Beat the egg yolks lightly and stir into the fondue. *Do not boil.* Remove the pan from the heat, add the sherry and whisked egg whites.

TO SERVE: Try florets of cauliflower to dip into the fondue.

Serves 4

Almond cheese fondue

IMPERIAL/METRIC	AMERICAN
1 clove garlic	1 clove garlic
¾ pint/4·5 dl dry white wine	2 cups dry white wine
12 oz/350 g Swiss cheese, grated	3 cups grated Swiss cheese
2 tablespoons cornflour	3 tablespoons cornstarch
1 oz/25 g butter	2 tablespoons butter
2 tablespoons kirsch	3 tablespoons kirsch
pinch nutmeg	pinch nutmeg
freshly ground black pepper	freshly ground black pepper
2 oz/50 g almonds, chopped	½ cup chopped almonds

Boil the garlic and wine until the liquid is reduced to approximately 12 fl oz (4 dl, 1½ cups). Remove the garlic. Mix the cheese and cornflour together and gradually add to the wine, allowing the cheese to melt, stirring. Add the butter and allow it to melt. Add the kirsch, nutmeg and black pepper. Toast almonds under a hot grill and stir into the fondue.

TO SERVE: Use cubes of ham and French bread to dip into the fondue.

Serves 4

Cider fondue

IMPERIAL/METRIC	AMERICAN
¾ pint/4·5 dl dry cider	2 cups cider
1½ lb/700 g Gruyère cheese, grated	6 cups grated Gruyère cheese
2 tablespoons flour	3 tablespoons all-purpose flour
3 tablespoons Calvados	4 tablespoons Calvados
salt and pepper	salt and pepper
pinch nutmeg	pinch nutmeg

Gently heat the cider in a fondue pan. Gradually add the cheese and flour, mixed together. Heat until all the cheese has melted, stirring constantly. Stir in the remaining ingredients and cook until the fondue has thickened.
TO SERVE: Cut apples in quarters and dip them in lemon juice. Serve these together with bread cubes to dip in the cider fondue.

Serves 6

Illustrated opposite

Asparagus fondue

IMPERIAL/METRIC	AMERICAN
¼ pint/1·5 dl dry white wine	⅔ cup dry white wine
1 lb/450 g Swiss cheese, grated	4 cups grated Swiss cheese
1 tablespoon cornflour	1 tablespoon cornstarch
1 (12-oz/340-g) can asparagus spears	1 (12-oz) can asparagus spears
2 tablespoons chopped parsley	3 tablespoons chopped parsley
freshly ground black pepper	freshly ground black pepper
cayenne pepper	cayenne pepper

Pour the wine into the fondue pan and heat gently. Gradually add the cheese and cornflour, mixed, and stir constantly until all the cheese has melted. Drain the asparagus and cut into 1-inch (2·5-cm) lengths. Stir into the fondue with the remaining ingredients.
TO SERVE: Use cubes of ham and French bread.

Serves 4

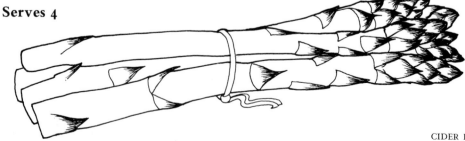

Blue cheese fondue

IMPERIAL/METRIC	AMERICAN
¾ pint/4·5 dl beer	2 cups beer
1 teaspoon grated onion	1 teaspoon grated onion
2 oz/50 g blue cheese, crumbled	½ cup crumbled blue cheese
12 oz/350 g Cheddar cheese, grated	3 cups grated Cheddar cheese
1 tablespoon flour	1 tablespoon all-purpose flour

Heat the beer and onion in a fondue pan. Add the blue cheese and stir until melted. Gradually stir in the Cheddar cheese and flour, mixed together, until all the cheese has melted and the fondue has thickened.
TO SERVE: Use cubes of pineapple or celery to dip into the fondue.

Serves 4

Onion and mushroom fondue

IMPERIAL/METRIC	AMERICAN
2 oz/50 g butter	¼ cup butter
2 shallots, finely chopped	2 shallots, finely chopped
2 oz/50 g mushrooms, chopped	½ cup chopped mushrooms
½ pint/3 dl white wine	1¼ cups white wine
12 oz/350 g Gruyère cheese, grated	3 cups grated Gruyère cheese
12 oz/350 g Emmenthal cheese, grated	3 cups grated Emmenthal cheese
pinch dry mustard	pinch dry mustard
pinch nutmeg	pinch nutmeg
1 tablespoon cornflour	1 tablespoon cornstarch
2 tablespoons kirsch	3 tablespoons kirsch
TO GARNISH:	TO GARNISH:
chopped parsley	chopped parsley

Melt the butter in a fondue pan and sauté the shallots and mushrooms for 5-10 minutes. Pour in the white wine and reheat gently. Gradually add the cheeses, stirring continuously until melted. Add the mustard and nutmeg. Blend the cornflour with kirsch and stir into the fondue. Cook for a further 10 minutes, stirring all the time until thickened. Garnish with the parsley.
TO SERVE: Try small button mushrooms, bread cubes and pickled onions to dip.

Serves 4-6

Champagne fondue

IMPERIAL/METRIC	AMERICAN
16 fl oz/0·5 litre champagne	2 cups champagne
1 lb/450 g Swiss cheese, grated	4 cups grated Swiss cheese
3 oz/75 g flour	¾ cup all-purpose flour
2 egg yolks	2 egg yolks
1 tablespoon cream	1 tablespoon cream
salt and pepper	salt and pepper

Heat the champagne slowly in a fondue pan. Stir in the cheese and flour, mixed, and cook until melted and smooth. Combine the egg yolks and cream and stir into the fondue. *Do not allow to boil.* Season to taste.
TO SERVE: Use cubes of ham, button mushrooms, French bread and chunks of cucumber to dip into this fondue.

Serves 4

Barbecued liver fondue

IMPERIAL/METRIC	AMERICAN
1 oz/25 g butter	2 tablespoons butter
1 medium-sized onion, chopped	1 medium-sized onion, chopped
1 oz/25 g flour	¼ cup all-purpose flour
8 fl oz/2·5 dl milk	1 cup milk
4 oz/100 g chicken livers, liquidised	¼ lb chicken livers, blended
1 tablespoon tomato purée	1 tablespoon tomato paste
2 tablespoons Worcestershire sauce	3 tablespoons Worcestershire sauce
salt and pepper	salt and pepper
2 oz/50 g Swiss cheese, grated	½ cup grated Swiss cheese
¼ pint/1·5 dl cream	⅔ cup cream

Melt the butter in a fondue pan and sauté the onion until softened. Stir in the flour and cook for 1-2 minutes. Add the milk, liver, tomato purée, Worcestershire sauce and seasoning. Stirring all the time, cook for 5-10 minutes. Gradually stir in the cheese and heat gently until melted. Add the cream and serve immediately.
TO SERVE: Use cubes of cucumber and bread, and pretzels to dip into the fondue.

Serves 4

Dutch fondue

1 clove garlic
¼ pint/1·5 dl white wine
1 teaspoon lemon juice
1 lb/450 g Gouda or Edam cheese, grated
1 tablespoon cornflour
1½ tablespoons brandy
freshly ground black pepper
pinch nutmeg

1 clove garlic
⅔ cup white wine
1 teaspoon lemon juice
4 cups grated Dutch cheese
1 tablespoon cornstarch
2 tablespoons brandy
freshly ground black pepper
pinch nutmeg

Rub the inside of a fondue pan with the cut clove of garlic. Add the wine and lemon juice and heat gently until almost boiling. Add the cheese, a little at a time, stirring continuously until completely melted. Blend the cornflour with the brandy and, when the mixture boils, stir this in. Add black pepper and nutmeg to season.
TO SERVE: Use cubes of French bread and sticks of celery to dip into the fondue.

Serves 4

Illustrated opposite

Caerphilly fondue

½ pint/3 dl beer
1 small onion, finely chopped
8 oz/225 g Caerphilly cheese, grated
2 tablespoons flour
1 tablespoon chopped chives
pinch celery salt
freshly ground black pepper

1¼ cups beer
1 small onion, finely chopped
2 cups grated Caerphilly cheese
3 tablespoons all-purpose flour
1 tablespoon chopped chives
pinch celery salt
freshly ground black pepper

Heat the beer and onion together in a saucepan, then strain the beer into a fondue pan. Gradually add the cheese and flour and, stirring continuously, allow the cheese to melt. Add the chives and season. Heat and stir the fondue until thickened and smooth.
TO SERVE: Use sticks of celery and carrot.
NOTE: This is not a stringy fondue.

Serves 2

Tomato and bacon fondue

IMPERIAL/METRIC	AMERICAN
1 clove garlic	1 clove garlic
8 oz/225 g Cheddar cheese, grated	2 cups grated Cheddar cheese
2 oz/50 g Gruyère cheese, grated	½ cup grated Gruyère cheese
¼ pint/1·5 dl condensed tomato soup	⅔ cup condensed tomato soup
1 teaspoon Worcestershire sauce	1 teaspoon Worcestershire sauce
3 tablespoons dry sherry	4 tablespoons dry sherry
4 tablespoons diced crisp bacon	⅓ cup diced crisp bacon
paprika pepper	paprika pepper

Rub the inside of a fondue pan with the cut clove of garlic. Add the cheeses, soup and sauce. Stir over a low heat until the cheese has melted. Stir in the sherry and bacon. Sprinkle the top with paprika pepper.
TO SERVE: Use frankfurter sausages to dip.

Serves 2-3

Mushroom fondue

IMPERIAL/METRIC	AMERICAN
2 oz/50 g butter	¼ cup butter
12 oz/350 g button mushrooms	3 cups button mushrooms
1 medium-sized onion, chopped	1 medium-sized onion, chopped
3 tablespoons flour	4 tablespoons all-purpose flour
8 fl oz/2·5 dl milk	1 cup milk
4 oz/100 g Swiss cheese, grated	1 cup grated Swiss cheese
4 fl oz/1·25 dl cream	½ cup cream
salt and pepper	salt and pepper
pinch dry mustard	pinch dry mustard

Melt the butter in a fondue pan and gently fry the mushrooms and onion for 10 minutes. Stir in the flour and milk, and bring to the boil. Cook for 1 minute. Add the cheese and stir until melted. Stir in the remaining ingredients. *Do not boil.*
TO SERVE: Use cubes of French bread to dip.

Serves 4

Tuna fondue

IMPERIAL/METRIC	AMERICAN
4 oz/100 g butter	$\frac{1}{2}$ cup butter
2 onions, chopped	2 onions, chopped
8 oz/225 g Cheddar cheese, grated	2 cups grated Cheddar cheese
6 tablespoons tomato ketchup	$\frac{1}{2}$ cup tomato catsup
2 tablespoons Worcestershire sauce	3 tablespoons Worcestershire sauce
2 tablespoons dry sherry	3 tablespoons dry sherry
1 (8-oz/227-g) can tuna fish	1 (8-oz) can tuna fish
2 tablespoons chopped parsley	3 tablespoons chopped parsley

Melt the butter in a fondue pan and sauté the onion until softened. Add the cheese, tomato ketchup, Worcestershire sauce and sherry. Cook the fondue, stirring continuously, until smooth and creamy, and all the cheese has melted. Drain the tuna, removing any bones, and flake. Stir the tuna and parsley into the fondue.

TO SERVE: Try cubes of cucumber, celery and French bread.

Serves 3-4

Game fondue

IMPERIAL/METRIC	AMERICAN
1 clove garlic	1 clove garlic
1 (15-oz/425 g) can game soup	1 (15-oz) can game soup
2 tablespoons cornflour	3 tablespoons cornstarch
$\frac{1}{4}$ teaspoon dry mustard	$\frac{1}{4}$ teaspoon dry mustard
10 oz/275 g Swiss cheese, grated	$2\frac{1}{2}$ cups grated Swiss cheese
pinch pepper	pinch pepper
1 tablespoon sherry	1 tablespoon sherry

Rub the inside of a fondue pan with the cut clove of garlic. Blend a little of the soup with the cornflour and mustard. Pour the remaining soup into the pan and stir in the blended cornflour. Add the cheese and stir over a low heat until melted. *Do not allow to boil.* Season with pepper and add the sherry.

TO SERVE: Use small artichoke hearts or bread cubes to dip into the fondue.

Serves 3-4

Swiss Cheddar fondue

IMPERIAL/METRIC	AMERICAN
1 clove garlic	1 clove garlic
¼ pint/1·5 dl dry white wine	⅔ cup dry white wine
8 oz/225 g Cheddar cheese, grated	2 cups grated Cheddar cheese
8 oz/225 g Gruyère cheese, grated	2 cups grated Gruyère cheese
1 teaspoon cornflour	1 teaspoon cornstarch
1 tablespoon lemon juice	1 tablespoon lemon juice
1 teaspoon castor sugar	1 teaspoon sugar
1 tablespoon kirsch	1 tablespoon kirsch
½ teaspoon dry mustard	½ teaspoon dry mustard
freshly ground black pepper	freshly ground black pepper

Rub the inside of a fondue pan with the cut clove of garlic. Pour all but 1 tablespoon of the wine into the pan and heat gently. Add the cheeses and stir well until melted.

Blend the remaining wine with the cornflour, lemon juice, sugar, kirsch, mustard and black pepper. Stir into the fondue and cook until thickened.

TO SERVE: Use cubes of French bread to dip into the fondue.

Serves 4

Illustrated opposite

Beer fondue

IMPERIAL/METRIC	AMERICAN
8 fl oz/2·5 dl beer	1 cup beer
8 oz/225 g Cheddar cheese, grated	2 cups grated Cheddar cheese
1 clove garlic, crushed	1 clove garlic, crushed
1 oz/25 g butter	2 tablespoons butter
2 tablespoons cornflour	3 tablespoons cornstarch
½ teaspoon dry mustard	½ teaspoon dry mustard
freshly ground black pepper	freshly ground black pepper

Place the beer, cheese and crushed garlic in a fondue pan. Cook gently, stirring, over a low heat until the cheese has melted. Stir in the butter.

Blend the cornflour and mustard in a little water and add to the fondue. Continue cooking until thickened, stirring all the time. Season with the pepper.

TO SERVE: Use pickled onions and French bread to dip into the fondue.

Serves 2

Fresh herb fondue

IMPERIAL/METRIC	AMERICAN
1 clove garlic	1 clove garlic
¼ pint/1·5 dl dry white wine	⅔ cup dry white wine
1 lb/450 g Gruyère cheese, grated	4 cups grated Gruyère cheese
3 teaspoons cornflour	3 teaspoons cornstarch
1 teaspoon chopped parsley	1 teaspoon chopped parsley
1 teaspoon chopped chives	1 teaspoon chopped chives
1 teaspoon chopped oregano	1 teaspoon chopped oregano
salt and pepper	salt and pepper
pinch nutmeg	pinch nutmeg

Rub the inside of a fondue pan with the cut clove of garlic. Pour in the wine, heating gently, then add the cheese. Stir continuously, until melted. Blend the cornflour with a little water and add to the fondue with the remaining ingredients. Heat until thickened, stirring.

TO SERVE: Use French bread and cubes of continental sausage to dip into the fondue.

Serves 4

Apple fondue

IMPERIAL/METRIC	AMERICAN
1 clove garlic	1 clove garlic
1 tablespoon cornflour	1 tablespoon cornstarch
¼ teaspoon dry mustard	¼ teaspoon dry mustard
¼ teaspoon paprika pepper	¼ teaspoon paprika pepper
¼ teaspoon nutmeg	¼ teaspoon nutmeg
¾ pint/4·5 dl apple juice	2 cups apple juice
1½ lb/700 g Cheddar cheese, grated	6 cups grated Cheddar cheese

Rub the inside of a fondue pan with a cut clove of garlic. Blend the cornflour, mustard, paprika, and nutmeg into a smooth paste with a little apple juice. Pour the remaining juice into the fondue pan and heat gently, adding the cheese gradually. Stir until the cheese has melted. Pour in the cornflour mixture, bring to the boil and simmer for 5 minutes, stirring continuously.

TO SERVE: Use chunks of apple dipped in lemon juice and toasted bread cubes.

Serves 4

Bacon and corn fondue

IMPERIAL/METRIC

¼ pint/1·5 dl white wine
1 lb/450 g Swiss cheese, grated
2 teaspoons cornflour
4 oz/100 g sweetcorn
3 oz/75 g bacon, chopped and fried
1 tablespoon chopped parsley
freshly ground black pepper

AMERICAN

⅔ cup white wine
4 cups grated Swiss cheese
2 teaspoons cornstarch
¾ cup corn kernels
½ cup chopped and fried bacon slices
1 tablespoon chopped parsley
freshly ground black pepper

Pour most of the wine into a fondue pan and heat gently. Gradually stir in the cheese, and cook until melted and smooth.

Blend the cornflour with the remaining wine and stir into the fondue with the sweetcorn, bacon, parsley and pepper.

TO SERVE: Use cubes of French bread to dip.

Serves 3-4

Avocado fondue

IMPERIAL/METRIC

1 oz/25 g butter
1 medium-sized onion, finely chopped
1 oz/25 g flour
8 fl oz/2·5 dl milk
salt and pepper
4 tablespoons lemon juice
1 medium-sized avocado, mashed or
    liquidised (skin and stone removed)
2 oz/50 g Swiss cheese, grated
¼ pint/1·5 dl cream
few drops Tabasco sauce

AMERICAN

2 tablespoons butter
1 medium-sized onion, finely chopped
¼ cup all-purpose flour
1 cup milk
salt and pepper
⅓ cup lemon juice
1 medium-sized avocado, mashed or
    blended (skin and pit removed)
½ cup grated Swiss cheese
⅔ cup cream
few drops Tabasco sauce

Melt the butter in a fondue pan, add the onion and sauté until softened. Stir in the flour and cook for 2 minutes. Remove from the heat and add all the remaining ingredients except the cheese, cream and Tabasco sauce. Cook gently for 5 minutes, stirring all the time, taking care not to boil the mixture. Add the cheese and stir until melted. Stir in the cream and Tabasco sauce, and serve immediately.

TO SERVE: Prawns are delicious to dip into this fondue.

Serves 4

Fondue Bourguignonne

Fondue bourguignonne is the name given to fondues in which pieces of meat or fish are cooked in hot oil or stock. The true fondue bourguignonne originates from the Burgundy district of France, and is the traditional beef fondue.

The type of pots used for these fondues are normally made from cast iron, copper or stainless steel. Only best quality meat should be used. If liked, it can be marinated before cooking, but do make sure the meat is dried well, as any liquid will cause the oil to spit. To save time, the oil or stock can be heated on top of the cooker before being brought to the table.

Each person is provided with a long fondue fork with which to hold the meat or fish in the hot cooking liquid. These forks often have different coloured handles so that everyone can easily identify their own. Care should be taken not to let the meat touch the bottom of the fondue pan, otherwise it will stick. When the meat has been cooked to required taste, it is removed from the oil or stock and dipped into the accompanying sauces.

There is a great variety of sauces in this section; choose those that complement or contrast the type of meat or fish you are using, but also include your favourites. Suggestions for sauces to accompany the fondues are given with each fondue recipe to help you choose.

A selection of four sauces to serve with each fondue is normally sufficient.

In this section a recipe for an Oriental fondue has been included. It is similar to the fondue bourguignonne, but the food is cooked in boiling stock instead of hot oil. The stock should be at boiling point before dipping in any meat or other chosen food.

FONDUE BOURGUIGNONNE (SEE RECIPE PAGE 36) WITH CUCUMBER AND SOURED CREAM SAUCE (PAGE 58), GREEN PEPPER AND GHERKIN SAUCE (PAGE 49) AND CHINESE SAUCE (PAGE 49)

Fondue bourguignonne

IMPERIAL/METRIC

1¼ lb/560 g fillet or rump steak
cooking oil

AMERICAN

1¼ lb beef filet or rump
cooking oil

Cut the beef into small cubes. Heat the oil in the fondue pan over a gentle heat. The oil should not come more than half way up the pan. Test the oil by dropping a small piece of bread in. If it turns brown within one minute the oil is ready for use. Keep the oil hot over a spirit burner on the table.

Place a portion of the cubed meat on individual plates for each person. The meat is then speared on to the end of a long fork and held in the oil until the meat is cooked to the individual's requirement. A variety of sauces such as cucumber and soured cream sauce (see page 58), green pepper and gherkin sauce (see page 49) and Chinese sauce (see page 49) can be served with the meat.

TO SERVE: Baked potatoes, salads, stuffed olives and French bread are ideal accompaniments.

NOTE: It may become necessary to adjust the heat if the oil becomes too cool or too hot. See page 9 for safety hints.

Serves 4

Illustrated on page 34

Lamb fondue

IMPERIAL/METRIC

6 oz/175 g good quality leg of lamb per person
cooking oil
MARINADE:
¼ pint/1·5 dl red wine
3 tablespoons oil
1 tablespoon chopped fresh herbs

AMERICAN

6 oz good quality leg of lamb per person
cooking oil
MARINADE:
⅔ cup red wine
4 tablespoons oil
1 tablespoon chopped fresh herbs

Cut the lamb into bite-sized pieces and marinate the lamb overnight, if possible. Drain and dry. Prepare and cook as for a fondue bourguignonne.
TO SERVE: Mint sauce (see page 53), orange and redcurrant sauce (see page 61), Cumberland sauce (see page 52) and onion sauce (see page 48) are most suitable to serve with this lamb fondue.

Oriental fondue

IMPERIAL/METRIC	AMERICAN
6 oz/175 g per person to include the following:	6 oz per person to include the following:
thin slices fillet beef, kidney, chicken, prawns, veal fillet	thin slices filet beef, kidney, chicken, shrimp, veal tenderloin
chicken stock	chicken stock
½-inch/1-cm piece fresh green ginger	½-inch piece fresh green ginger

Arrange the meat, offal, poultry and shellfish on a large serving dish. Heat the chicken stock, bring to the boil and pour into a fire kettle or fondue pan. Add the piece of green ginger.

Each person selects from the dish and spears the chosen food on the end of a fondue fork. The food is then dipped into the boiling stock to cook. (The stock should be kept at boiling point throughout the meal.)

TO SERVE: Make a selection of sauces such as almond sauce (see page 59), pepper sauce (see page 45), Mexican mayonnaise (see page 47) and curried cheese sauce (see page 45); together with fried rice and a salad.

NOTE: When the meal is finished, a little sherry is added to the chicken stock and then served as soup, if liked.

Fish fondue

IMPERIAL/METRIC	AMERICAN
6 oz/175 g raw white fish per person	6 oz raw white fish per person
FISH STOCK:	FISH STOCK:
fish trimmings, bones, etc.	fish trimmings, bones, etc.
1 onion, chopped	1 onion, chopped
2 carrots, chopped	2 carrots, chopped
bouquet garni	bouquet garni
few sprigs parsley	few sprigs parsley
salt and pepper	salt and pepper
½ pint/3 dl dry white wine	1¼ cups dry white wine

Prepare the fish and cut into bite-sized pieces. For the fish stock, place the fish trimmings and bones into a saucepan, add the vegetables together with the bouquet garni and parsley. Cover with water, bring to the boil and remove the scum. Cover and simmer for 30 minutes. Strain, season and add the wine. Pour into a fondue pan and reheat.

Spear the fish on fondue forks and cook in the boiling wine stock.

TO SERVE: Make a selection of sauces such as anchovy mayonnaise (see page 44), curry sauce (see page 58), thousand island dressing (see page 51) and lemon sauce (see page 61).

Spicy meat balls

IMPERIAL/METRIC	AMERICAN
1 onion, finely chopped	1 onion, finely chopped
1 tablespoon oil	1 tablespoon oil
1 lb/450 g minced beef	1 lb ground beef
salt and pepper	salt and pepper
¼ teaspoon grated nutmeg	¼ teaspoon grated nutmeg
¼ teaspoon garlic salt	¼ teaspoon garlic salt
1 egg, beaten	1 egg, beaten
flour	flour
cooking oil	cooking oil

Sauté the onion in the hot oil until soft – about 5-10 minutes. Mix with the minced beef, salt, pepper, nutmeg, garlic salt and beaten egg. Flour the hands and shape the mixture into walnut-sized balls.

Fill a fondue pan half full with oil and heat. Spear each meat ball on a long fondue fork and allow it to cook in the heated oil.

TO SERVE: A bowl of mustard, bought peach chutney, chutney sauce and mango chutney.

Serves 4-6

Illustrated opposite

Potato fondue

IMPERIAL/METRIC	AMERICAN
20 small new potatoes	20 small new potatoes
salt	salt
6 fl oz/2 dl oil	¾ cup oil
½ pint/3 dl cider vinegar	1¼ cups cider vinegar
1 large onion, finely chopped	1 large onion, finely chopped
freshly ground black pepper	freshly ground black pepper

Cook the potatoes in boiling salted water. Combine the oil, vinegar, onion and seasoning in a fondue pan and cook until the onion is soft. Dip the hot cooked potatoes into the sauce.

TO SERVE: Make a selection of sauces such as orange and redcurrant sauce (see page 61), pepper sauce (see page 45) and Tijuana sauce (see page 47).

Serves 4

Kidney fondue

IMPERIAL/METRIC

12 lambs' kidneys
flour
cooking oil

AMERICAN

12 lamb kidneys
flour
cooking oil

Skin the kidneys, split them open and remove the cores. Cut into quarters and dredge lightly with flour. Heat the oil in a fondue pan and continue as for a fondue bourguignonne (see page 36).

TO SERVE: Make a selection of sauces, such as mushroom sauce (see page 53), onion sauce (see page 48), Cumberland sauce (see page 52) and a spicy pepper sauce (see page 54).

Serves 4

Pork fondue

IMPERIAL/METRIC

2 lb/1 kg pork fillet
cooking oil

AMERICAN

2 lb pork tenderloin
cooking oil

Cut the pork into 1-inch (2·5-cm) cubes. Heat the oil in a fondue pan and continue as for fondue bourguignonne (see page 36).

TO SERVE: Make a selection of sauces such as apple sauce (see page 60), curry sauce (see page 58) and sweet 'n' sour sauce (see page 44).

Serves 4

Shellfish fondue

IMPERIAL/METRIC

6-8 oz/175-225 g large prawns or
    scampi per person
cornflour
beaten egg
fresh white breadcrumbs
cooking oil

AMERICAN

6-8 oz large prawns or jumbo
    shrimp per person
cornstarch
beaten egg
fresh white bread crumbs
cooking oil

Peel the prawns or scampi, and remove the veins. Toss in cornflour, then coat in beaten egg and fresh breadcrumbs. Heat the oil. Spear the

prawns or scampi on to fondue forks and dip into the hot oil to cook.
TO SERVE: Tartare sauce (see page 43) and avocado dressing (see page 51) make delicious accompanying sauces.

Vegetable fritter fondue

IMPERIAL/METRIC

SUITABLE FOODS:
button mushrooms
sprigs of cauliflower
banana slices dipped in lemon juice
canned pineapple cubes, drained
cubes of Cheddar cheese
tiny par-boiled new potatoes
slices of courgette
apple slices dipped in lemon juice
FRENCH BATTER:
4 oz/100 g plain flour
½ teaspoon salt
1 tablespoon corn oil
¼ pint/1·5 dl water
2 egg whites

cooking oil

AMERICAN

SUITABLE FOODS:
button mushrooms
sprigs of cauliflower
banana slices dipped in lemon juice
canned pineapple cubes, drained
cubes of Cheddar or similar cheese
tiny par-boiled new potatoes
slices of zucchini
apple slices dipped in lemon juice
FRENCH BATTER:
1 cup all-purpose flour
½ teaspoon salt
1 tablespoon corn oil
⅔ cup water
2 egg whites

cooking oil

Make sure that all the foods are in fairly small pieces so they will cook quickly, and that they are free of excess moisture.

Make the batter by mixing the flour and salt with the oil and water, and beat until smooth. Whisk the egg whites until stiff and fold into the batter just before required.

Fill a fondue pan about half full with oil and heat. Secure a piece of food on a long fondue fork and dip into the French batter, coating the food completely. Cook in the heated oil until the batter is crisp and golden brown.
TO SERVE: Serve these fritters with a selection of sauces such as anchovy mayonnaise (see page 44), soured cream sauce (see page 45) and mustard; a green salad and French bread.

Serves 4

Illustrated on page 42

Sauces

Basic mayonnaise sauce

IMPERIAL/METRIC

2 egg yolks
pinch dry mustard
salt and pepper
½ teaspoon sugar
few drops lemon juice
¼ pint/3 dl oil
2-3 tablespoons wine vinegar

AMERICAN

2 egg yolks
pinch dry mustard
salt and pepper
½ teaspoon sugar
few drops lemon juice
1¼ cups oil
3-4 tablespoons wine vinegar

Combine the egg yolks, seasonings, sugar and lemon juice in a bowl using a wooden spoon. Add the oil drop by drop, whisking well until the mixture becomes thick. Beat in the vinegar – this will thin down the mayonnaise – and adjust the seasoning.

Variations
CURRY MAYONNAISE: Add sufficient curry paste or curry powder to taste.
HERB MAYONNAISE: Add 1 teaspoon of mixed fresh herbs.
TARTARE SAUCE: Add 3 tablespoons (U.S. 4 tablespoons) chopped capers, 3 tablespoons (U.S. 4 tablespoons) chopped gherkins and chopped parsley.
EGG AND TOMATO MAYONNAISE: Add 1 chopped hard-boiled egg and 2 skinned and chopped tomatoes.

Curried barbecue sauce

IMPERIAL/METRIC

8 tablespoons mayonnaise (see above)
4 tablespoons tomato ketchup
1-2 teaspoons lemon juice
1 teaspoon Worcestershire sauce
1 teaspoon grated onion
1 teaspoon curry powder
½ teaspoon cayenne pepper
few drops Tabasco sauce

AMERICAN

⅔ cup mayonnaise (see above)
5 tablespoons tomato catsup
1-2 teaspoons lemon juice
1 teaspoon Worcestershire sauce
1 teaspoon grated onion
1 teaspoon curry powder
½ teaspoon cayenne pepper
few drops Tabasco sauce

Combine all the ingredients together in a bowl, taking care not to add too much Tabasco sauce, as it is very hot. Serve cold.
An ideal sauce to serve with a fondue bourguignonne (see page 36).

Sweet 'n' sour sauce

IMPERIAL/METRIC	AMERICAN
2 oz/50 g butter	¼ cup butter
2 onions, chopped	2 onions, chopped
2 rashers bacon, chopped	2 bacon slices, chopped
2 tablespoons tomato purée	3 tablespoons tomato paste
½ pint/3 dl dry cider	1¼ cups dry cider
¼ pint/1·5 dl water	⅔ cup water
1 tablespoon demerara sugar	1 tablespoon light brown sugar
salt and pepper	salt and pepper
2 tablespoons Worcestershire sauce	3 tablespoons Worcestershire sauce
2 tablespoons mango chutney	3 tablespoons mango chutney
3 teaspoons arrowroot	3 teaspoons arrowroot flour
2 tablespoons water	3 tablespoons water

Melt the butter and fry the onions and bacon until soft, but not browned. Add the remaining ingredients except for the arrowroot and water. Bring to the boil, stirring, and simmer for 15-20 minutes. Stir in the blended arrowroot and water and cook for 1 minute.

Anchovy mayonnaise

IMPERIAL/METRIC	AMERICAN
½ pint/3 dl mayonnaise (see page 43)	1¼ cups mayonnaise (see page 43)
2 teaspoons anchovy essence	2 teaspoons anchovy extract
1 (2-oz/50-g) can anchovies, drained and chopped	1 (2-oz) can anchovies, drained and chopped
1 tablespoon chopped parsley	1 tablespoon chopped parsley
1 clove garlic, crushed	1 clove garlic, crushed
4 black olives, stoned and chopped	4 ripe olives, pitted and chopped
1 hard-boiled egg, chopped	1 hard-cooked egg, chopped
2 tablespoons cream	3 tablespoons cream
salt and pepper	salt and pepper

Place all the ingredients in a mixing bowl and combine thoroughly. Serve cold.

This mayonnaise is an ideal accompaniment to a fish fondue (see page 37), shellfish fondue (see page 40) or a vegetable fritter fondue (see page 41).

Pepper sauce

IMPERIAL/METRIC

1 oz/25 g butter
2 green peppers, deseeded and chopped
1 onion, finely chopped
4 tablespoons water
4 tomatoes, skinned and chopped
few drops Tabasco sauce
salt and pepper

AMERICAN

2 tablespoons butter
2 green sweet peppers, deseeded and chopped
1 onion, finely chopped
5 tablespoons water
4 tomatoes, skinned and chopped
few drops Tabasco sauce
salt and pepper

Melt the butter in a saucepan and sauté the peppers and onion until golden brown. Add the remaining ingredients and bring to the boil, stirring continuously. Simmer for 10-15 minutes. Serve hot.

Soured cream sauce

IMPERIAL/METRIC

¼ pint/1·5 dl thick soured cream
pinch salt
¼ teaspoon French mustard
pinch castor sugar

AMERICAN

⅔ cup thick sour cream
pinch salt
¼ teaspoon French mustard
pinch sugar

Combine all the ingredients together in a bowl. If the sauce is too thick, stir in a little cream from the top of the milk or single cream. Chill well before serving.

Illustrated on page 42

Curried cheese sauce

IMPERIAL/METRIC

8 oz/225 g cream cheese
4 tablespoons mayonnaise (see page 43)
¼ pint/1·5 dl natural yogurt
3 teaspoons curry powder
2 teaspoons grated onion
salt and pepper

AMERICAN

1 cup cream cheese
5 tablespoons mayonnaise (see page 43)
⅔ cup unflavored yogurt
3 teaspoons curry powder
2 teaspoons grated onion
salt and pepper

Blend the cheese, mayonnaise and yogurt together in a bowl until smooth. Stir in the curry powder, grated onion and seasoning. Chill well.

Blender barbecue sauce

IMPERIAL/METRIC	AMERICAN
1 small onion, chopped	1 small onion, chopped
1 clove garlic, crushed	1 clove garlic, crushed
8 fl oz/2·5 dl red wine	1 cup red wine
1 teaspoon Worcestershire sauce	1 teaspoon Worcestershire sauce
4 fl oz/1·25 dl water	½ cup water
1 tablespoon wine vinegar	1 tablespoon wine vinegar
few drops chilli sauce	few drops chili sauce
1 tablespoon brown sugar	1 tablespoon brown sugar
salt	salt
freshly ground black pepper	freshly ground black pepper
1 tablespoon redcurrant jelly	1 tablespoon red currant jelly
few drops Tabasco sauce	few drops Tabasco sauce
2 teaspoons cornflour blended with 1 tablespoon water	2 teaspoons cornstarch blended with 1 tablespoon water

Place all the ingredients in a saucepan and bring to the boil, stirring. Simmer for 5-10 minutes. Cool for a few minutes. Blend the sauce in a liquidiser and return the sauce to the saucepan. Bring to the boil and reheat.

Hollandaise sauce

IMPERIAL/METRIC	AMERICAN
8 oz/225 g butter	1 cup butter
1 tablespoon water	1 tablespoon water
1 teaspoon wine vinegar	1 teaspoon wine vinegar
4 egg yolks	4 egg yolks
2 tablespoons lemon juice	3 tablespoons lemon juice
salt	salt
freshly ground black pepper	freshly ground black pepper

Melt the butter in a saucepan, taking care not to let it brown. Add the water and vinegar. Put the egg yolks, lemon juice, salt and freshly ground black pepper in a liquidiser. Using a slow speed, pour in the melted butter mixture in a steady stream. The sauce should become thick. Reheat if necessary in a bowl placed over a saucepan of hot water. If the sauce should become too thick, beat in a few drops of warm water.

Mexican mayonnaise

IMPERIAL/METRIC

8 fl oz/2·5 dl mayonnaise (see page 43)
2 fl oz/1 dl chilli sauce or according to taste
1½ tablespoons tomato purée
1 teaspoon Worcestershire sauce
1 tablespoon chopped fresh tarragon
1 tablespoon chopped chives
salt and pepper

AMERICAN

1 cup mayonnaise (see page 43)
¼ cup chili sauce or according to taste
2 tablespoons tomato paste
1 teaspoon Worcestershire sauce
1 tablespoon chopped fresh tarragon
1 tablespoon chopped chives
salt and pepper

Combine the mayonnaise, chilli sauce, tomato purée and Worcestershire sauce in a bowl. Fold in the tarragon and chopped chives, and season the mayonnaise to taste. Serve cold.

Tijuana sauce

IMPERIAL/METRIC

4 fl oz/1·25 dl soy sauce
2 tablespoons chilli sauce
2 tablespoons dry sherry
4 oz/100 g crunchy peanut butter
4 spring onions, sliced
few drops lemon juice

AMERICAN

½ cup soy sauce
3 tablespoons chili sauce
3 tablespoons dry sherry
½ cup crunchy peanut butter
4 scallions, sliced
few drops lemon juice

Mix together the soy sauce, chilli sauce and sherry. Gradually blend this into the peanut butter in a bowl. Fold in the sliced spring onions and add a few drops of lemon juice. Chill before serving.
NOTE: This sauce is very hot.

Cucumber and dill sauce

IMPERIAL/METRIC

¼ pint/1·5 dl soured cream
1 tablespoon white vinegar
½ cucumber, deseeded and diced
¼ teaspoon dried dill or 2 teaspoons
   chopped fresh dill
salt
pinch cayenne pepper

AMERICAN

⅔ cup sour cream
1 tablespoon white vinegar
½ cucumber, deseeded and diced
¼ teaspoon dried dill or 2 teaspoons
   chopped fresh dill
salt
pinch cayenne pepper

Mix together the soured cream and vinegar in a bowl. Add the diced cucumber and the dill, and season the sauce to taste. Serve this sauce well chilled.

Tarragon sauce

IMPERIAL/METRIC

8 fl oz/2·5 dl mayonnaise (see page 43)
2 tablespoons soured cream
pinch mustard
2 teaspoons tarragon vinegar
salt and pepper
½ teaspoon dried tarragon

AMERICAN

1 cup mayonnaise (see page 43)
3 tablespoons sour cream
pinch mustard
2 teaspoons tarragon vinegar
salt and pepper
½ teaspoon dried tarragon

Combine all the ingredients together in a bowl and chill well.
   This sauce goes well with a pork fondue (see page 40).

Onion sauce

IMPERIAL/METRIC

1 large onion, finely chopped
½ pint/3 dl béchamel sauce (see page 52)
pinch nutmeg
salt and pepper

AMERICAN

1 large onion, finely chopped
1¼ cups béchamel sauce (see page 52)
pinch nutmeg
salt and pepper

Cook the onion in boiling salted water until soft. Drain well. Combine the béchamel sauce, nutmeg and seasoning with the onion in a bowl.
   Serve hot or cold with a lamb fondue (see page 36), fondue bourguignonne (see page 36) or a kidney fondue (see page 40).

Chinese sauce

1 red pepper, deseeded
1 small onion
2 tablespoons oil
6 fl oz/2 dl chicken stock
¼ pint/1·5 dl pineapple juice
½ teaspoon soy sauce
2 pieces stem ginger, finely chopped
4 oz/100 g canned sweetcorn
1 tablespoon cornflour
2 tablespoons water

AMERICAN

1 red sweet pepper, deseeded
1 small onion
3 tablespoons oil
¾ cup chicken stock
⅔ cup pineapple juice
½ teaspoon soy sauce
2 pieces stem ginger, finely chopped
¾ cup canned corn kernels
1 tablespoon cornstarch
3 tablespoons water

Chop the pepper and onion, and sauté in the oil until softened. Add all the
remaining ingredients except the cornflour and water and simmer for
10 minutes. Blend the cornflour and water, and stir into the sauce. Bring
to the boil and cook for 1 minute. Serve hot.

Illustrated on page 35

Green pepper and gherkin sauce

IMPERIAL/METRIC

1 onion, chopped
2 green peppers, chopped
4 large gherkins, sliced
1 oz/25 g butter
4 tablespoons water
salt and pepper
¼ teaspoon chilli sauce

AMERICAN

1 onion, chopped
2 green sweet peppers, chopped
4 large dill pickles, sliced
2 tablespoons butter
5 tablespoons water
salt and pepper
¼ teaspoon chili sauce

Sauté the onion, green pepper and gherkins together in the butter until
golden. Add the remaining ingredients, bring to the boil and simmer for
10 minutes, stirring occasionally.

Illustrated on page 34

Avocado dressing

IMPERIAL/METRIC	AMERICAN
1 ripe avocado	1 ripe avocado
8 fl oz/2·5 dl mayonnaise (see page 43)	1 cup mayonnaise (see page 43)
¼ pint/1·5 dl soured cream	⅔ cup sour cream
2 tablespoons chopped parsley	3 tablespoons chopped parsley
1 tablespoon wine vinegar	1 tablespoon wine vinegar
1 tablespoon tarragon vinegar	1 tablespoon tarragon vinegar
1 tablespoon finely chopped onion	1 tablespoon finely chopped onion
1 tablespoon lemon juice	1 tablespoon lemon juice
pinch salt	pinch salt
freshly ground black pepper	freshly ground black pepper

Peel the avocado and remove the stone. Chop the flesh and combine thoroughly with the remaining ingredients. Chill for several hours before using.

Illustrated opposite

Thousand island dressing

IMPERIAL/METRIC	AMERICAN
½ onion, grated	½ onion, grated
1 stick celery, finely chopped	1 stalk celery, finely chopped
1 tablespoon chopped parsley	1 tablespoon chopped parsley
¼ green pepper, chopped	¼ green sweet pepper, chopped
1 tablespoon chopped green olives	1 tablespoon chopped green olives
½ pint/3 dl mayonnaise (see page 43)	1¼ cups mayonnaise (see page 43)
1 hard-boiled egg, chopped	1 hard-cooked egg, chopped
3 teaspoons tomato purée	3 teaspoons tomato paste

Combine all the ingredients together thoroughly and chill.
    This dressing is especially good served with a fish fondue (see page 37).

Variation
Add ¼ teaspoon curry powder or paste, or more according to taste.

Illustrated opposite

Cumberland sauce

IMPERIAL/METRIC	AMERICAN
1 oz/25 g brown sugar	2 tablespoons brown sugar
salt and pepper	salt and pepper
pinch cayenne pepper	pinch cayenne pepper
2 tablespoons cornflour	3 tablespoons cornstarch
$\frac{1}{2}$ pint/3 dl red wine	$1\frac{1}{4}$ cups red wine
4 tablespoons cold water	$\frac{1}{3}$ cup cold water
5 oz/150 g redcurrant jelly	$\frac{1}{2}$ cup red currant jelly
grated rind and juice of $\frac{1}{2}$ orange	grated rind and juice of $\frac{1}{2}$ orange
few drops lemon juice	few drops lemon juice
pinch sugar	pinch sugar

Combine the brown sugar, seasoning, cayenne pepper and cornflour with a little wine. Heat the remaining wine and pour over the cornflour. Return to the pan and gently bring to the boil. Simmer 2-3 minutes until thickened. Add the remaining ingredients and heat until the redcurrant jelly has melted.

Béchamel sauce

IMPERIAL/METRIC	AMERICAN
$\frac{1}{2}$ pint/3 dl milk	$1\frac{1}{4}$ cups milk
1 onion, halved	1 onion, halved
1 carrot, sliced	1 carrot, sliced
bouquet garni	bouquet garni
sprig parsley	sprig parsley
1 oz/25 g butter	2 tablespoons butter
1 oz/25 g flour	$\frac{1}{4}$ cup all-purpose flour
salt and pepper	salt and pepper

Place the milk, onion, carrot, bouquet garni and parsley in a saucepan and bring to the boil. Remove from the heat and allow to infuse for 30 minutes. Strain.

Melt the butter in a clean saucepan, add the flour and cook, stirring all the time, for 1 minute. Remove from the heat and gradually stir in the strained milk. Return to the heat and slowly bring to the boil. Simmer for 3-4 minutes and season according to taste.

Serve as an accompaniment to a fish fondue (see page 37).

Mushroom sauce

IMPERIAL/METRIC	AMERICAN
4 oz/100 g mushrooms	1 cup mushrooms
2 oz/50 g butter	¼ cup butter
salt and pepper	salt and pepper
1 oz/25 g flour	¼ cup all-purpose flour
¼ pint/1·5 dl milk	⅔ cup milk
1 tablespoon sherry	1 tablespoon sherry

Cut the mushrooms into thin slices. Melt the butter in a saucepan and sauté the mushrooms together with the seasoning. Stir in the flour and cook for 1 minute. Add the milk and bring to the boil, stirring. Add the sherry and serve.

Peanut sauce

IMPERIAL/METRIC	AMERICAN
1 onion, chopped	1 onion, chopped
1 clove garlic, crushed	1 clove garlic, crushed
2 oz/50 g butter	¼ cup butter
1 tablespoon Worcestershire sauce	1 tablespoon Worcestershire sauce
3 tablespoons peanut butter	4 tablespoons peanut butter
1 tablespoon lemon juice	1 tablespoon lemon juice
¼ pint/1·5 dl soured cream	⅔ cup sour cream

Sauté the onion and garlic in the melted butter until golden. Add the Worcestershire sauce, peanut butter and lemon juice. Cool, then add the soured cream.

Mint sauce

IMPERIAL/METRIC	AMERICAN
2-3 tablespoons chopped fresh mint leaves	3-4 tablespoons chopped fresh mint leaves
2 teaspoons sugar	2 teaspoons sugar
1 tablespoon boiling water	1 tablespoon boiling water
¼ pint/1·5 dl vinegar	⅔ cup vinegar

Sprinkle the chopped mint with sugar and pour over the boiling water. Add the vinegar and allow to stand for 30 minutes before serving.

Spicy pepper sauce

IMPERIAL/METRIC	AMERICAN
½ oz/15 g butter	1 tablespoon butter
1 medium-sized onion, chopped	1 medium-sized onion, chopped
1 clove garlic, crushed	1 clove garlic, crushed
1 medium-sized pepper, deseeded and chopped	1 medium-sized sweet pepper, deseeded and chopped
2 tablespoons tomato purée	3 tablespoons tomato paste
½ teaspoon marjoram	½ teaspoon marjoram
¼ teaspoon thyme	¼ teaspoon thyme
½ pint/3 dl chicken stock	1¼ cups chicken stock
few drops Tabasco sauce	few drops Tabasco sauce
pinch sugar	pinch sugar
freshly ground black pepper	freshly ground black pepper
1 teaspoon cornflour	1 teaspoon cornstarch

Melt the butter in a saucepan and fry the onion until softened. Add the garlic and pepper and cook for 2-3 minutes. Stir in all the remaining ingredients except the cornflour. Bring to the boil and simmer for 20 minutes. Blend the cornflour with a little water and pour into the sauce. Stir and cook for 1 minute.

Horseradish sauce

IMPERIAL/METRIC	AMERICAN
½ pint/3 dl milk	1¼ cups milk
1 onion	1 onion
few peppercorns	few peppercorns
bay leaf	bay leaf
1 oz/25 g butter	2 tablespoons butter
1 oz/25 g flour	¼ cup all-purpose flour
salt and pepper	salt and pepper
2 tablespoons finely grated fresh horseradish	3 tablespoons finely grated fresh horseradish
1 teaspoon wine vinegar	1 teaspoon wine vinegar
2 tablespoons single cream	3 tablespoons half and half

Heat the milk in a saucepan together with the onion, peppercorns and bay leaf. Bring to the boil and then remove from the heat. Allow to infuse for 30 minutes.

Strain the milk into a clean saucepan. Add the butter and flour, and whisking all the time over a gentle heat, bring to the boil. Season.

Stir the horseradish into the sauce with the wine vinegar and cream. *Do not allow to boil.*

Chive sauce

IMPERIAL/METRIC

2 egg yolks
2 tablespoons lemon juice
pinch dry mustard
pinch salt
12 fl oz/4 dl oil
3 tablespoons chopped chives
3 tablespoons chopped parsley
1 tablespoon chopped onion

AMERICAN

2 egg yolks
3 tablespoons lemon juice
pinch dry mustard
pinch salt
1⅓ cups oil
4 tablespoons chopped chives
4 tablespoons chopped parsley
1 tablespoon chopped onion

Place the egg yolks, lemon juice, mustard and salt in a liquidiser and blend for a few seconds. Add the oil, a little at a time, until the mixture thickens. Pour into a bowl and stir in the remaining ingredients. Chill.

Danish blue sauce

IMPERIAL/METRIC

2 oz/50 g Danish blue cheese, crumbled
4 fl oz/1·25 dl soured cream
few drops lemon juice
1 tablespoon finely chopped onion

AMERICAN

½ cup crumbled Danish blue cheese
½ cup sour cream
few drops lemon juice
1 tablespoon finely chopped onion

Combine all the ingredients together thoroughly in a bowl and chill.

This sauce makes an unusual, exciting accompaniment to a fondue bourguignonne (see page 36).

Illustrated on page 50

Cream cheese sauce

IMPERIAL/METRIC	AMERICAN
8 oz/225 g cream cheese	1 cup cream cheese
1 teaspoon grated lemon rind	1 teaspoon grated lemon rind
pinch salt	pinch salt
6 tablespoons olive oil	$\frac{1}{2}$ cup olive oil
1 teaspoon chopped fresh chervil or $\frac{1}{2}$ teaspoon dried chervil	1 teaspoon chopped fresh chervil or $\frac{1}{2}$ teaspoon dried chervil

Blend the cheese with the lemon rind and salt in a bowl. Gradually beat in the oil until all has been absorbed. Mix in the chervil and chill well.

Rémoulade sauce

IMPERIAL/METRIC	AMERICAN
8 fl oz/2·5 dl mayonnaise (see page 43)	1 cup mayonnaise (see page 43)
1 tablespoon chopped capers	1 tablespoon chopped capers
1 tablespoon chopped gherkins	1 tablespoon chopped dill pickles
1 clove garlic, crushed	1 clove garlic, crushed
1 tablespoon chopped parsley	1 tablespoon chopped parsley
pinch tarragon	pinch tarragon
few drops anchovy essence	few drops anchovy extract

Combine all the ingredients together in a bowl and chill well.
Serve with fish fondue (see page 37) or shellfish fondue (see page 40).

Hot chilli sauce

IMPERIAL/METRIC	AMERICAN
8 oz/225 g tomato purée	1 cup tomato paste
1 small chilli, deseeded	1 small chili, deseeded
2 teaspoons olive oil	2 teaspoons olive oil
2 teaspoons red wine vinegar	2 teaspoons red wine vinegar
pinch oregano	pinch oregano
pinch ground cumin	pinch ground cumin
pinch salt	pinch salt
freshly ground black pepper	freshly ground black pepper

Place all the ingredients in a liquidiser and blend for a few seconds, until the sauce is smooth. Pour into a bowl and serve cold.

Peppered cucumber relish

IMPERIAL/METRIC	AMERICAN
1 oz/25 g butter	2 tablespoons butter
1 medium-sized onion, finely chopped	1 medium-sized onion, finely chopped
1 green pepper, deseeded and chopped	1 green sweet pepper, deseeded and chopped
3-inch/8-cm piece of cucumber, chopped	3-inch piece of cucumber, chopped
$\frac{1}{2}$ pint/3 dl stock	$1\frac{1}{4}$ cups stock
2 teaspoons cornflour	2 teaspoons cornstarch
2 tablespoons water	3 tablespoons water
salt and pepper	salt and pepper

Melt the butter in a saucepan and sauté the onion and pepper for 5 minutes. Add the cucumber and stock. Bring to the boil and simmer for 10–15 minutes. Blend the cornflour with the water and stir into the sauce. Cook until thickened, stirring. Season to taste.

Serve with a fondue bourguignonne (see page 36).

Illustrated on the jacket

Béarnaise sauce

IMPERIAL/METRIC	AMERICAN
1 onion, finely chopped	1 onion, finely chopped
3 tablespoons white wine	4 tablespoons white wine
2 teaspoons tarragon vinegar	2 teaspoons tarragon vinegar
1 teaspoon dried tarragon	1 teaspoon dried tarragon
pinch salt	pinch salt
freshly ground black pepper	freshly ground black pepper
$\frac{1}{2}$ bay leaf	$\frac{1}{2}$ bay leaf
few drops lemon juice	few drops lemon juice
$\frac{1}{2}$ pint/3 dl hollandaise sauce (see page 46)	$1\frac{1}{4}$ cups hollandaise sauce (see page 46)

Place the onion, wine, vinegar, tarragon, salt, pepper, bay leaf and lemon juice in a small saucepan. Bring to the boil and reduce the liquid to 1 tablespoon.

Place the hollandaise sauce in a liquidiser, add the tablespoon of reduced liquid and blend.

Cucumber and soured cream sauce

IMPERIAL/METRIC	AMERICAN
$\frac{1}{2}$ cucumber	$\frac{1}{2}$ cucumber
$\frac{1}{4}$ pint/1·5 dl soured cream	$\frac{2}{3}$ cup sour cream
4 tablespoons mayonnaise (see page 43)	5 tablespoons mayonnaise (see page 43)
salt and pepper	salt and pepper
few drops lemon juice	few drops lemon juice
1 tablespoon chopped chives	1 tablespoon chopped chives

Peel the cucumber and dice. Combine all the other ingredients in a bowl and fold in the diced cucumber. Serve cold.

Illustrated on page 34

Curry sauce

IMPERIAL/METRIC	AMERICAN
1 oz/25 g butter	2 tablespoons butter
1 carrot, chopped	1 carrot, chopped
1 onion, chopped	1 onion, chopped
1 small potato, sliced	1 small potato, sliced
1–2 tablespoons curry powder	1–3 tablespoons curry powder
1 teaspoon tomato purée	1 teaspoon tomato paste
$\frac{1}{2}$ pint/3 dl stock	$1\frac{1}{4}$ cups stock
2 oz/50 g desiccated coconut	$\frac{2}{3}$ cup shredded coconut

Melt the butter in a saucepan and sauté the carrot, onion and potato for 5 minutes. Stir in the curry powder and cook for 1 minute. Add the tomato purée and stock. Simmer for 10 minutes.

Place the slightly cooled sauce in a liquidiser and blend for a few seconds. Return the sauce to the saucepan, stir in the coconut, and reheat.

Almond sauce

IMPERIAL/METRIC	AMERICAN
2 oz/50 g butter	¼ cup butter
3 oz/75 g flour	¾ cup all-purpose flour
¼ pint/1·5 dl single cream	⅔ cup half and half
1 pint/6 dl chicken stock	2½ cups chicken stock
4 oz/100 g almonds, slivered	1 cup slivered almonds
3 oz/75 g stuffed olives, sliced	½ cup sliced stuffed olives
1 tablespoon lemon juice	1 tablespoon lemon juice

Melt the butter in a saucepan and stir in the flour, cook for 1 minute. Add 1 tablespoon of the cream and the stock, stirring continuously. Bring to the boil. Add the remaining cream with the rest of the ingredients. Reheat, but do not boil. Serve with oriental or fish fondue (see page 37).

Pickled mustard sauce

IMPERIAL/METRIC	AMERICAN
4 tablespoons mayonnaise (see page 43)	5 tablespoons mayonnaise (see page 43)
2 tablespoons piccalilli	3 tablespoons piccalilli
½ teaspoon made mustard	½ teaspoon prepared mustard
pinch castor sugar	pinch sugar
curry powder to taste	curry powder to taste

Combine together the mayonnaise, piccalilli, mustard and sugar. Add curry powder. Serve with a fondue bourguignonne (see page 36).

Illustrated on the jacket

Cumberland mayonnaise

IMPERIAL/METRIC	AMERICAN
8 fl oz/2·5 dl mayonnaise	1 cup mayonnaise
4 oz/100 g redcurrant jelly	⅓ cup red currant jelly
2 tablespoons creamed horseradish relish	3 tablespoons creamed horseradish relish
salt and pepper	salt and pepper
2 tablespoons chopped parsley	3 tablespoons chopped parsley
4 fl oz/1·25 dl double cream	½ cup heavy cream

Place all the ingredients, except the cream, in a bowl and mix well together. Whip the cream lightly and fold into the mixture. Chill.

Cranberry and lemon sauce

IMPERIAL/METRIC	AMERICAN
8 oz/225 g cranberries	½ lb cranberries
4 oz/100 g sugar	½ cup sugar
3 tablespoons water	4 tablespoons water
few drops lemon juice	few drops lemon juice

Place the cranberries, sugar and water in a saucepan. Bring to the boil and simmer for 15 minutes. Sieve the cranberry mixture or place in a liquidiser and blend for a few seconds. Add a few drops of lemon juice to taste. Allow to chill before serving.

This sauce is a delicious accompaniment to an oriental fondue (see page 37).

Apple sauce

IMPERIAL/METRIC	AMERICAN
4 fl oz/1·25 dl apple purée	½ cup applesauce
4 fl oz/1·25 dl mayonnaise (see page 43)	½ cup mayonnaise (see page 43)
grated rind of ½ lemon	grated rind of ½ lemon
few drops lemon juice	few drops lemon juice
freshly ground black pepper	freshly ground black pepper

Combine all the ingredients together in a bowl and chill well.

This sauce makes an ideal accompaniment to a pork fondue (see page 40).

Black cherry sauce

IMPERIAL/METRIC	AMERICAN
1 lb/450 g black cherries	1 lb bing cherries
2 oz/50 g raisins	6 tablespoons raisins
¼ pint/1·5 dl water	⅔ cup water
few drops lemon juice	few drops lemon juice
sugar to taste	sugar to taste

Place all the ingredients in a saucepan and bring to the boil. Simmer gently for 15-20 minutes. Sieve and serve hot.

This is an ideal sauce to accompany a lamb fondue (see page 36), pork fondue (see page 40) or a fondue bourguignonne (see page 36).

Lemon sauce

IMPERIAL/METRIC

1½ oz/40 g butter
1½ oz/40 g flour
½ pint/3 dl milk
grated rind of 1 lemon
1 tablespoon lemon juice
1 tablespoon cream
1 tablespoon chopped parsley
pinch sugar
salt and pepper

AMERICAN

3 tablespoons butter
6 tablespoons all-purpose flour
1¼ cups milk
grated rind of 1 lemon
1 tablespoon lemon juice
1 tablespoon cream
1 tablespoon chopped parsley
pinch sugar
salt and pepper

Melt the butter in a pan, stir in the flour and cook for 1 minute. Gradually stir in the milk and bring to the boil. Add the remaining ingredients, stirring, but do not boil. Serve immediately.

Serve with a fish fondue (see page 37) or a shellfish fondue (see page 40).

Orange and redcurrant sauce

IMPERIAL/METRIC

1 small onion, finely chopped
grated rind and juice of 1 large orange
grated rind and juice of 1 lemon
6 tablespoons redcurrant jelly
4 teaspoons arrowroot

AMERICAN

1 small onion, finely chopped
grated rind and juice of 1 large orange
grated rind and juice of 1 lemon
7 tablespoons red currant jelly
4 teaspoons arrowroot flour

Place the onion in a small saucepan of boiling salted water and cook for 5 minutes. Drain.

Place the orange and lemon rinds and juice into a saucepan with the redcurrant jelly. Bring to the boil and simmer for 2 minutes. Blend the arrowroot with a little water and add to the sauce, together with the onion. Bring to the boil, stirring, and allow to thicken.

Dessert Fondues

This type of fondue is probably less well known than the fondues mentioned earlier; but they are now becoming increasingly popular. Like the others, dessert fondues are great fun to prepare and, of course, to eat! It is recommended that a heavy-based pot or pan is used and the heat is kept to a minimum. A candle flame is normally sufficient for this purpose, or a spirit burner may be used. There is a great variety of 'dippers' or 'dunkers' one can choose – cubes of sponge cake, marshmallows, fresh fruit, small meringues, small choux buns and many others as you will see in the recipes. This type of fondue is not only popular with children, but also the adults, especially those with a sweet tooth!

As the names suggest, dessert fondues are usually served as a sweet, but should never follow a fondue if it has been served as the main dish. When serving a dessert fondue for children, always make sure it is properly supervised and that adults are present.

A dessert fondue follows the same principles as the cheese fondue. Each person is provided with a long fondue fork and a plate, selects the dipper, spears it on to the end of the fork and then dips into the dessert fondue – the perfect way to end a meal, include in a buffet or simply serve with coffee.

Cherry fondue

IMPERIAL/METRIC

2 (14-oz/396-g) cans cherry pie filling
3 tablespoons cream
4 tablespoons sweet white wine
few drops almond essence

AMERICAN

2 (14-oz) cans cherry pie filling
4 tablespoons cream
⅓ cup sweet white wine
few drops almond extract

Place the cherry pie filling in a fondue pan and heat gently. Stir in the cream, sweet white wine and almond essence. Heat gently.
TO SERVE: Use macaroons to dip.

Serves 4

Illustrated on page 62

Ice cream fondue

IMPERIAL/METRIC

1 (11-oz/312-g) packet coffee ice cream
1 tablespoon brandy
1 tablespoon cornflour

AMERICAN

1 (11-oz) package coffee ice cream
1 tablespoon brandy
1 tablespoon cornstarch

Melt the ice cream and stir in the mixed brandy and cornflour.
TO SERVE: Slice chunks of banana, sprinkled with lemon juice, to dip.

Serves 2

Creamy banana fondue

IMPERIAL/METRIC

3 bananas
1 tablespoon sugar
5 tablespoons cream
2 oz/50 g chocolate, grated

AMERICAN

3 bananas
1 tablespoon sugar
6 tablespoons cream
3 squares chocolate, grated

Liquidise or sieve the bananas, place in a fondue pan and heat gently. Add the sugar and cream and, when simmering, gradually add the chocolate.
TO SERVE: Use apple or pineapple pieces to dip.

Serves 2

Mallow fondue

IMPERIAL/METRIC	AMERICAN
1 (6-oz/175-g) packet marshmallows	1 (6-oz) package marshmallows
3 tablespoons cream or milk	4 tablespoons cream or milk
few drops lemon juice	few drops lemon juice
1 oz/25 g almonds, chopped	¼ cup chopped almonds

Place the marshmallows and cream or milk in a fondue pan placed over a low heat. Allow the marshmallows to melt, stirring. Add the lemon juice and nuts, and allow the mixture to become quite hot.
TO SERVE: Use sponge fingers to dip.

Serves 2

Snowflake fondue

IMPERIAL/METRIC	AMERICAN
9 oz/250 g white chocolate	9 oz white chocolate
4 fl oz/1·25 dl cream	½ cup cream
1 tablespoon kirsch	1 tablespoon kirsch

Heat the chocolate and cream in a fondue pan, stirring continuously, but do not boil. When melted, stir in the kirsch. Serve as above.

Serves 2

Dark orange fondue

IMPERIAL/METRIC	AMERICAN
8 oz/225 g plain chocolate	½ lb semi-sweet chocolate
¼ pint/1·5 dl orange squash	⅔ cup undiluted orange drink
1 tablespoon arrowroot	1 tablespoon arrowroot flour
1 tablespoon apricot brandy	1 tablespoon apricot brandy

Melt the chocolate in a fondue pan over a low heat. Blend the orange squash with the arrowroot and add to the chocolate, stirring. Simmer for 2 minutes then add the brandy.
TO SERVE: Use macaroons to dip.

Serves 2

Mocha fondue

IMPERIAL/METRIC

8 oz/225 g plain chocolate
1 tablespoon instant coffee powder
6 fl oz/2 dl fresh double cream
1 tablespoon sherry

AMERICAN

½ lb semi-sweet chocolate
1 tablespoon instant coffee powder
¾ cup whipping or heavy cream
1 tablespoon sherry

Grate the chocolate and mix with the coffee powder. Place the cream in a fondue pan and add the chocolate and coffee. Heat gently, stirring until smooth and blended. Add the sherry. Swirl with cream.
TO SERVE: Use cubes of plain cake, sponge fingers or marshmallows to dip.

Serves 4

Illustrated opposite

Dark fudge fondue

IMPERIAL/METRIC

1 oz/25 g butter
3 oz/75 g dark soft brown sugar
6 fl oz/2 dl milk
1 tablespoon black treacle
1 tablespoon cornflour blended with
  2 tablespoons water

AMERICAN

2 tablespoons butter
6 tablespoons dark brown sugar
¾ cup milk
1 tablespoon molasses
1 tablespoon cornstarch blended with
  3 tablespoons water

Place the butter and sugar in a saucepan and heat gently until the sugar dissolves. Bring to the boil and simmer for 1 minute, stirring. Add the milk, treacle and blended cornflour and water. Again, bring to the boil, stirring continuously, and simmer for 2-3 minutes. Pour into a fondue pan and serve hot.
TO SERVE: Use sponge fingers and plain biscuits to dip.

Serves 2

Apricot fondue

IMPERIAL/METRIC

1 lb/450 g dried apricots
8 oz/225 g castor sugar
pinch cinnamon
3 tablespoons apricot brandy

AMERICAN

3 cups dried apricots
1 cup sugar
pinch cinnamon
4 tablespoons apricot brandy

Soak the apricots until soft, then simmer them in a little water until tender. Purée the apricots in a liquidiser.

Place the purée in a fondue pan, together with the sugar, cinnamon and a little water if the mixture is very thick. Heat; stir in the apricot brandy just before serving.

TO SERVE: Use macaroons and pieces of plain sponge to dip.

Serves 4

Blackberry fondue

IMPERIAL/METRIC

6 fl oz/2 dl water
4 oz/100 g sugar
8 oz/225 g blackberries
2 tablespoons brandy
¼ pint/1·5 dl single cream

AMERICAN

¾ cup water
½ cup sugar
2 cups blackberries
3 tablespoons brandy
⅔ cup half and half

Place the water and sugar in a pan and heat to dissolve the sugar. Add the blackberries and simmer until soft. Sieve the fruit. Stir in the brandy and reheat in the fondue pan. Remove from the heat and stir in the cream.

TO SERVE: Use slices of apple or cubes of plain cake to dip.

Serves 4

Spiced fondue

IMPERIAL/METRIC

8 oz/225 g plain chocolate
4 fl oz/1·25 dl cream
¼ teaspoon ground nutmeg
¼ teaspoon ground cinnamon
grated rind of ½ orange

AMERICAN

½ lb semi-sweet chocolate
½ cup cream
¼ teaspoon ground nutmeg
¼ teaspoon ground cinnamon
grated rind of ½ orange

Grate the chocolate and place in a fondue pan. Add the cream and spices. Heat gently, stirring all the time. Stir in the orange rind just before serving. *Do not boil.*

TO SERVE: Use macaroons and sponge fingers to dip.

Serves 4

Orange fondue

IMPERIAL/METRIC	AMERICAN
5 oz/150 g castor sugar	good ½ cup sugar
1 tablespoon cornflour	1 tablespoon cornstarch
¾ pint/4·5 dl fresh orange juice	2 cups fresh orange juice
2 oz/50 g butter	¼ cup butter
grated rind of 1 orange	grated rind of 1 orange
1 teaspoon grated lemon rind	1 teaspoon grated lemon rind
2 tablespoons brandy	3 tablespoons brandy

Place the sugar and cornflour in the top of a double saucepan. Gradually stir in the orange juice. Heat gently, stirring all the time, until thickened. Remove from the heat and stir in the remaining ingredients. Serve warm in a fondue pan.

TO SERVE: Use plain sweet biscuits or sponge fingers to dip.

Serves 4

Raspberry fondue

IMPERIAL/METRIC	AMERICAN
1 (15-oz/425-g) can raspberries	1 (15-oz) can raspberries
1 tablespoon cornflour	1 tablespoon cornstarch
4 fl oz/1·25 dl double cream	½ cup heavy cream
½ teaspoon lemon juice	½ teaspoon lemon juice

Drain the raspberries and sieve them (reserving the juice). Add sufficient juice to make the raspberry purée up to ½ pint (3 dl, 1¼ cups) and pour into a fondue pan. Combine the cornflour with a little of the remaining juice, then place in a fondue pan with the remaining ingredients. Heat gently, stirring, until the fondue is smooth and thickened. *Do not boil.*

TO SERVE: Use cubes of plain cake to dip into this fruit fondue.

Serves 4

Tabletop Cookery

The recipes in this section are designed so that they can either be cooked entirely at the table or partially cooked beforehand, so that they can be finished off at the table.

For tabletop cookery you will require one of the following: an electric frying pan, toaster oven, chafing dish, flambé pan, omelette pan, or a heavy-based casserole.

Probably the most famous dish that is cooked in this way is crêpes Suzette; but tabletop cookery is, of course, not limited to desserts as you will find in this section – recipes are given for both savoury and sweet dishes. The preparation for this type of cooking has to be done carefully, but the result is very spectacular and is an ideal way of entertaining if you are out to impress your guests. Do not be over-ambitious – only attempt one tabletop dish at any one meal.

A flambéed dish is always very exciting. When doing this, use a lighted match or taper. Allow the spirit used to warm slightly. Pour over the food, ignite and serve when the flames have died down. To encourage the flaming of a sweet tabletop dessert, sprinkle with a little castor sugar before adding the warmed spirit and igniting.

PARTY FARE: PARTY KEBABS (SEE RECIPE PAGE 73), BARBECUED SAUSAGES (SEE RECIPE PAGE 89), PEANUT HAMBURGERS (SEE RECIPE PAGE 92) AND CIDER CUP (SEE RECIPE PAGE 122)

Savoury tabletop dishes

Swiss rosti

IMPERIAL/METRIC	AMERICAN
2 lb/1 kg potatoes	2 lb potatoes
2 oz/50 g butter	¼ cup butter
pinch salt	salt
freshly ground black pepper	freshly ground black pepper
6 oz/175 g Swiss cheese, grated	1½ cups grated Swiss cheese

Scrub the potatoes and blanch in boiling water for 5-7 minutes. Drain and allow them to cool. Remove the skins and coarsely grate the potatoes.

Melt the butter in a large frying pan. Add the grated potato, seasoning and cheese and fry over a gentle heat for 10-15 minutes. Turn the potato mixture over and allow it to become crisp and brown underneath. Loosen the 'rosti' around the edge with a palette knife. Invert a warmed plate on top and turn the cooked mixture out in one piece.

Serve as an accompaniment to any meat or fish dish.

Serves 4

Chicken flambé

IMPERIAL/METRIC	AMERICAN
1 small chicken, cooked	1 small chicken, cooked
2 oz/50 g butter	¼ cup butter
salt and pepper	salt and pepper
2 tablespoons chopped fresh parsley	3 tablespoons chopped fresh parsley
3 tablespoons brandy	4 tablespoons brandy
¼ pint/1·5 dl cream	⅔ cup cream
2 egg yolks	2 egg yolks

Cut the chicken into quarters. Melt the butter in a frying pan and lightly brown the chicken. Season and continue to cook over a low heat for 15-20 minutes. Add the parsley and brandy and ignite with a lighted match. Mix the cream and egg yolks and pour over the chicken. Serve immediately.

Serves 4

Party kebabs

IMPERIAL/METRIC	AMERICAN
8 button mushrooms	8 button mushrooms
8 oz/225 g leg of lamb, cubed	8 oz leg of lamb, cubed
½ green pepper, sliced	½ green sweet pepper, sliced
4 bay leaves	4 bay leaves
2 large tomatoes, quartered	2 large tomatoes, quartered
2 tablespoons oil	3 tablespoons oil
1 teaspoon mixed herbs	1 teaspoon mixed herbs

Thread the mushrooms, lamb, pepper, bay leaves and tomatoes equally on to 4 long skewers. Combine the oil and herbs and brush over the kebabs. Place the kebabs in a toaster oven, turning frequently and brushing with the oil, as required.

Serve with a bowl of cooked, cold rice which has been tossed in French dressing and garnished with strips of red pepper and chopped parsley, and salad.

Serves 4

Illustrated on page 70

Liver in wine

IMPERIAL/METRIC	AMERICAN
12 thin slices calves' liver	12 thin slices calves' liver
seasoned flour	seasoned flour
2 oz/50 g butter	¼ cup butter
2 onions, sliced	2 onions, sliced
pinch dried tarragon	pinch dried tarragon
½ pint/3 dl red wine	1¼ cups red wine
salt and pepper	salt and pepper
1 tablespoon chopped parsley	1 tablespoon chopped parsley

Toss the liver in seasoned flour. Melt half the butter in a frying pan and sauté the onion. Remove the onion from the pan and add the remaining butter to the pan. Sauté the liver with the tarragon for 3 minutes on each side. Remove and keep the liver hot.

Pour the wine into the pan, bring to the boil, and reduce until there is half the quantity left. Add seasoning. Replace the onions and lightly-cooked liver. Sprinkle with chopped parsley and serve with creamed potatoes.

Serves 6

CHILLI CON CARNE
(SEE RECIPE PAGE 76)

Escalopes l'orange

IMPERIAL/METRIC	AMERICAN
2 oz/50 g butter	$\frac{1}{4}$ cup butter
4 veal escalopes	4 veal scallops
$\frac{1}{2}$ oz/15 g flour	2 tablespoons all-purpose flour
2 oranges	2 oranges
2 tablespoons sherry	3 tablespoons sherry
$\frac{1}{4}$ pint/1·5 dl stock	$\frac{2}{3}$ cup stock
TO GARNISH:	TO GARNISH:
watercress	watercress

Heat the butter and brown the escalopes on both sides. Remove them from the pan and stir in the flour. Cook for 1 minute. Stir in the rind and juice of 1 orange, the sherry and stock. Bring to the boil, replace the escalopes and simmer for 5-10 minutes. Slice the remaining orange and use to garnish the veal, together with the watercress.

Serves 4

Chilli con carne

IMPERIAL/METRIC	AMERICAN
1 tablespoon oil	1 tablespoon oil
1 onion, chopped	1 onion, chopped
1 clove garlic, crushed	1 clove garlic, crushed
$\frac{1}{2}$ green pepper, chopped	$\frac{1}{2}$ green sweet pepper, chopped
1 lb/450 g minced beef	2 cups ground beef
1 (15$\frac{1}{4}$-oz/432-g) can tomato soup	1 (15$\frac{1}{4}$-oz) can tomato soup
1 tablespoon chilli powder	1 tablespoon chili powder
1 (10-oz/280-g) can kidney beans, drained	1 (10-oz) can kidney beans, drained
salt and pepper	salt and pepper
$\frac{1}{4}$ pint/1·5 dl water	$\frac{2}{3}$ cup water
1 bay leaf	1 bay leaf

Heat the oil in a flameproof dish and sauté the onion, garlic and pepper for 2-3 minutes. Add the minced beef and brown. Stir in the soup, chilli powder, beans, seasoning and water. Add the bay leaf. Bring to the boil, stirring, and simmer for 20-30 minutes. Remove the bay leaf and serve with boiled rice.

Serves 4

Illustrated on pages 74-75

Veal bonne femme

IMPERIAL/METRIC	AMERICAN
1½ oz/40 g butter	3 tablespoons butter
4 veal chops	4 veal chops
4 oz/100 g lean bacon	¼ lb lean bacon
8 oz/225 g button onions	½ lb tiny onions
4 oz/100 g button mushrooms	1 cup button mushrooms
½ oz/15 g flour	2 tablespoons all-purpose flour
5 tablespoons white wine	½ cup white wine
¾ pint/4·5 dl stock	2 cups stock
salt and pepper	salt and pepper
bouquet garni	bouquet garni
TO GARNISH:	TO GARNISH:
watercress	watercress

Heat the butter and brown the chops on both sides. Remove them from the pan.

Cut the bacon into strips and fry them in the butter, together with the onions and mushrooms, until golden brown. Stir in the flour and cook for 1 minute. Pour in the wine and stock. Bring to the boil, stirring, season and replace the chops. Add the bouquet garni and simmer for 10–15 minutes. Garnish with watercress.

Serves 4

Mexican mince

IMPERIAL/METRIC	AMERICAN
½ oz/15 g butter	1 tablespoon butter
8 oz/225 g minced beef	1 cup ground beef
¼ pint/1·5 dl stock	⅔ cup stock
1 clove garlic, crushed	1 clove garlic, crushed
2 tablespoons tomato purée	3 tablespoons tomato paste
few drops Tabasco sauce	few drops Tabasco sauce
salt and pepper	salt and pepper
1 (7¾-oz/220-g) can baked beans	1 (7¾-oz) can baked beans

Melt the butter in a flameproof dish, add the beef and brown quickly. Add the remaining ingredients and simmer gently for 15–20 minutes. Serve with boiled rice.

Serves 2

Steak Diane

IMPERIAL/METRIC	AMERICAN
4 oz/100 g butter	½ cup butter
1 clove garlic, crushed	1 clove garlic, crushed
1 onion, chopped	1 onion, chopped
4 oz/100 g mushrooms, sliced	1 cup sliced mushrooms
4 thin slices rump or fillet steak	4 thin slices rump or filet steak
brandy	brandy
freshly ground black pepper	freshly ground black pepper
1 tablespoon chopped fresh parsley	1 tablespoon chopped fresh parsley

Heat the butter in a heavy-based copper pan and sauté the garlic, onion and mushrooms until softened. Place the steaks in the same pan and seal quickly on both sides. (Cook the steaks to required taste.) Pour in a little brandy and ignite with a lighted match. Serve immediately, sprinkled with freshly ground black pepper and chopped parsley.

Serves 4

Illustrated opposite

Salami omelette

IMPERIAL/METRIC	AMERICAN
2 tomatoes	2 tomatoes
1 small onion	1 small onion
1 potato, cooked	1 potato, cooked
2 oz/50 g salami	8 slices salami
½ green pepper	½ green sweet pepper
4 eggs	4 eggs
salt and pepper	salt and pepper
1 teaspoon oil	1 teaspoon oil
TO GARNISH:	TO GARNISH:
chopped parsley	chopped parsley

Peel and chop the tomatoes. Dice the onion, cooked potato, salami and pepper. Beat the eggs together with the seasoning and add the diced vegetables and salami.

Heat the oil in an omelette pan, pour in the egg mixture and cook for 3-4 minutes. Brown the surface of the omelette under a preheated grill. Serve immediately, sprinkled with parsley.

Serves 2

Eggs in a nest

IMPERIAL/METRIC	AMERICAN
I clove garlic, crushed	I clove garlic, crushed
I onion, chopped	I onion, chopped
4 tomatoes, skinned and chopped	4 tomatoes, skinned and chopped
2 oz/50 g butter	¼ cup butter
pinch dried basil	pinch dried basil
I tablespoon Worcestershire sauce	I tablespoon Worcestershire sauce
¼ pint/1·5 dl water	⅔ cup water
salt and pepper	salt and pepper
4 eggs	4 eggs

Sauté the garlic, onion and tomatoes in melted butter in a flameproof dish for 5-10 minutes. Add the basil, Worcestershire sauce, water and seasoning. Break the eggs on top and cook gently until set. Serve immediately.

Serves 4

Frikadella

IMPERIAL/METRIC	AMERICAN
8 oz/225 g beef, minced	I cup ground beef
8 oz/225 g lean pork, minced	I cup lean ground pork
I onion, grated	I onion, grated
I egg	I egg
salt and pepper	salt and pepper
2-3 tablespoons milk	3-4 tablespoons milk
flour	flour
2-3 oz/50-75 g butter for frying	4-6 tablespoons butter for frying

Mix the meat with the grated onion. Stir in the egg, seasoning, milk and enough flour to make a fairly soft mixture. Divide the mixture into eight and shape into flat rounds.

Melt the butter in a frying pan and fry the meat rounds on both sides until browned – approximately 20 minutes. Serve with cooked fresh vegetables.

Serves 4

Sautéed aubergines

IMPERIAL/METRIC	AMERICAN
2 aubergines	2 eggplants
salt and pepper	salt and pepper
2 oz/50 g butter	¼ cup butter
1 clove garlic, crushed	1 clove garlic, crushed
¼ pint/1·5 dl soured cream	⅔ cup sour cream
2 teaspoons paprika pepper	2 teaspoons paprika pepper
freshly ground black pepper	freshly ground black pepper
TO GARNISH:	TO GARNISH:
chopped parsley	chopped parsley

Slice the aubergines, sprinkle with salt and leave for 20–30 minutes. Rinse well.

Melt the butter in a flameproof dish and sauté the garlic and aubergines for 2–3 minutes on each side. Pour over the cream and sprinkle over the paprika and black pepper. Garnish with chopped parsley.

Serve as a starter at a dinner party.

Serves 4

Savoury cod

IMPERIAL/METRIC	AMERICAN
4 (6-oz/175-g) cod portions	4 (6-oz) cod portions
1 onion, chopped	1 onion, chopped
1 clove garlic, crushed	1 clove garlic, crushed
1 oz/25 g butter	2 tablespoons butter
2 tablespoons tomato purée	3 tablespoons tomato paste
salt and pepper	salt and pepper
½ pint/3 dl stock	1¼ cups stock
2 tablespoons capers	3 tablespoons capers

Wash and trim the fish. Fry the onion and garlic in melted butter, in a flameproof dish, until transparent. Stir in the tomato purée and seasoning. Place the fish in the tomato mixture and pour over the stock. Simmer gently until the fish is tender. Stir in the capers and serve with rice.

Serves 4

Paella

IMPERIAL/METRIC	AMERICAN
2 oz/50 g butter	¼ cup butter
4 chicken portions, cooked, skinned and boned	4 chicken portions, cooked, skinned and boned
1 onion, chopped	1 onion, chopped
1 clove garlic, crushed	1 clove garlic, crushed
2 pints/generous litre chicken stock	5 cups chicken stock
4 oz/100 g long-grain rice	scant ½ cup long-grain rice
blade saffron or pinch turmeric	blade saffron or pinch turmeric
1 (6-oz/170-g) jar mussels	1 (6-oz) jar mussels
8 oz/225 g peas	½ lb peas
1 green pepper, sliced	1 green sweet pepper, sliced
8 oz/225 g shelled prawns	½ lb shelled prawns or shrimp

Heat the butter in a large flameproof dish and sauté the chicken, onion and garlic until golden brown. Pour in 1 pint (6 dl, 2½ cups) of the chicken stock. Bring to the boil and simmer for 15 minutes.

Add the rice, saffron or turmeric and the rest of the stock, together with all the remaining ingredients except the prawns. Simmer for 15 minutes, adding the prawns for the last 5 minutes, or until the rice is cooked and stock absorbed. Serve immediately, sprinkled with parsley.

Serves 4

Illustrated opposite

Piperade

IMPERIAL/METRIC	AMERICAN
1 tablespoon oil	1 tablespoon oil
1 green pepper, deseeded and sliced	1 green sweet pepper, deseeded and sliced
4 tomatoes, skinned, deseeded and chopped	4 tomatoes, skinned, deseeded and chopped
1 small onion, sliced	1 small onion, sliced
salt and pepper	salt and pepper
3 tablespoons cubed ham	4 tablespoons cubed smoked ham
4 eggs	4 eggs

Heat the oil in a frying pan and gently sauté the sliced pepper, tomatoes and onion until softened. Season and stir in the ham.

Beat the eggs and pour over the vegetables. Stir gently until the mixture is like soft scrambled egg. Serve on savoury biscuits

Serves 2

Chicken suprême

IMPERIAL/METRIC	AMERICAN
I (3-lb/1·5-kg) chicken	I (3-lb) chicken
2 oz/50 g butter	¼ cup butter
I stick celery, finely chopped	I stalk celery, finely chopped
I onion, finely chopped	I onion, finely chopped
I carrot, finely chopped	I carrot, finely chopped
2 tablespoons chopped parsley	3 tablespoons chopped parsley
sprig fresh tarragon	sprig fresh tarragon
5 tablespoons whisky	6 tablespoons whiskey
¼ pint/1·5 dl single cream	⅔ cup half and half
freshly ground black pepper	freshly ground black pepper

Skin the chicken and remove the flesh, keeping it in fairly large portions. Melt the butter in a frying pan and sauté the vegetables with the parsley and tarragon. Add the chicken pieces and cook until tender, stirring occasionally. Add the whisky, pour over the cream and sprinkle with black pepper.

Serves 4

Sautéed chicken livers

IMPERIAL/METRIC	AMERICAN
12 oz/350 g chicken livers	¾ lb chicken livers
½ oz/15 g seasoned flour	2 tablespoons seasoned flour
2 oz/50 g butter	¼ cup butter
2 oz/50 g streaky bacon, chopped	¼ cup chopped bacon slices
2 tablespoons Marsala	3 tablespoons Marsala
6 tablespoons stock	½ cup stock
2 teaspoons tomato purée	2 teaspoons tomato paste
I tablespoon chopped parsley	I tablespoon chopped parsley

Cut the chicken livers into small pieces and toss in the seasoned flour. Melt the butter in a flameproof dish and sauté the bacon and the livers for 3 minutes. Stir in the Marsala, stock, tomato purée and parsley, and simmer for 5 minutes. Serve with buttered noodles.

Serves 4

Haddock and prawn provencal

IMPERIAL/METRIC	AMERICAN
1 clove garlic, crushed	1 clove garlic, crushed
2 onions, sliced	2 onions, sliced
3 tablespoons oil	4 tablespoons oil
1 lb/450 g tomatoes, skinned	1 lb tomatoes, skinned
1 tablespoon chopped parsley	1 tablespoon chopped parsley
grated rind and juice of 1 lemon	grated rind and juice of 1 lemon
1½ lb/700 g haddock	1½ lb haddock
4 oz/100 g prawns	⅔ cup prawns or shrimp
salt and pepper	salt and pepper

Fry the garlic and onion in the oil in a flameproof dish, together with the chopped tomatoes, for 8-10 minutes. Add the parsley, lemon rind and juice.

Cut the fish into bite-sized pieces and add to the sauce. Simmer until cooked – about 15-20 minutes, then stir in the prawns and season to taste. Cook for a further 5 minutes. Serve with rice.

Serves 4-6

Spanish omelette

IMPERIAL/METRIC	AMERICAN
1 small onion, chopped	1 small onion, chopped
1 clove garlic, crushed	1 clove garlic, crushed
1 oz/25 g butter	2 tablespoons butter
3 potatoes, cooked and chopped	3 potatoes, cooked and chopped
1 tomato, skinned and chopped	1 tomato, skinned and chopped
1 green pepper, blanched and sliced	1 green sweet pepper, blanched and sliced
pinch mixed herbs	pinch mixed herbs
3 eggs	3 eggs
salt and pepper	salt and pepper

Sauté the onion and garlic in the butter in an omelette pan. Add the potatoes, tomato, pepper and herbs. Beat the eggs and pour over the vegetables. Season. Stir gently and cook until the eggs are set.

Serves 2

HEREFORD PORK CHOPS
(SEE RECIPE PAGE 88)

86

Hereford pork chops

IMPERIAL/METRIC	AMERICAN
2 tablespoons oil	3 tablespoons oil
4 pork chops	4 pork chops
2 onions, sliced	2 onions, sliced
1 clove garlic, crushed	1 clove garlic, crushed
2–3 carrots, sliced	2–3 carrots, sliced
2 sticks celery, sliced	2 stalks celery, sliced
$\frac{1}{2}$ oz/15 g flour	2 tablespoons all-purpose flour
1 tablespoon tomato purée	1 tablespoon tomato paste
$\frac{1}{4}$ pint/1·5 dl cider	$\frac{2}{3}$ cup cider
$\frac{1}{2}$ pint/3 dl stock	$1\frac{1}{4}$ cups stock
bouquet garni	bouquet garni
few sprigs fresh rosemary	few sprigs fresh rosemary
1 tablespoon chopped parsley	1 tablespoon chopped parsley

Heat the oil in a flameproof dish or frying pan and brown the chops on both sides. Remove from the pan, add the onions, garlic, carrots and celery and fry until golden. Stir in the flour, tomato purée, cider, stock, bouquet garni, rosemary and parsley. Replace the chops, bring to the boil and simmer gently for 40 minutes.

Serves 4

Illustrated on pages 86–87

Barbecued beans

IMPERIAL/METRIC	AMERICAN
1 oz/25 g butter	2 tablespoons butter
4 oz/100 g streaky bacon, chopped	$\frac{1}{2}$ cup chopped bacon slices
1 onion, chopped	1 onion, chopped
1 ($15\frac{3}{4}$-oz/437-g) can baked beans	1 ($15\frac{3}{4}$-oz) can baked beans
1 tablespoon tomato purée	1 tablespoon tomato paste
1 tablespoon Worcestershire sauce	1 tablespoon Worcestershire sauce
salt and pepper	salt and pepper

Melt the butter in a frying pan and sauté the bacon and onion until golden brown. Add the remaining ingredients and simmer for 5-10 minutes. Serve on buttered toast.

Serves 4

Sweet 'n' sour gammon

IMPERIAL/METRIC	AMERICAN
1 oz/25 g butter	2 tablespoons butter
2 gammon rashers	2 uncooked smoked ham slices
2 tablespoons wine vinegar	3 tablespoons wine vinegar
2 tablespoons redcurrant jelly	3 tablespoons red currant jelly
1 teaspoon French mustard	1 teaspoon French mustard
1 tablespoon brown sugar	1 tablespoon brown sugar
freshly ground black pepper	freshly ground black pepper

Heat the butter in a frying pan. Snip the edges of the gammon rashers and fry them on both sides until brown – about 10-15 minutes. Remove them from the pan and keep hot.

Place the remaining ingredients in the pan and stir until heated through. Replace the gammon rashers and reheat. Serve sprinkled with chopped parsley.

Serves 2

Barbecued sausages

IMPERIAL/METRIC	AMERICAN
1 lb/450 g cocktail sausages	1 lb small link sausages or frankfurters
1 tablespoon oil	1 tablespoon oil
1 small onion, chopped	1 small onion, chopped
1 teaspoon vinegar	1 teaspoon vinegar
1 tablespoon Worcestershire sauce	1 tablespoon Worcestershire sauce
1 teaspoon brown sugar	1 teaspoon brown sugar
1 tablespoon redcurrant jelly	1 tablespoon red currant jelly
$\frac{1}{2}$ pint/3 dl tomato juice	$1\frac{1}{4}$ cups tomato juice
2 teaspoons cornflour	2 teaspoons cornstarch
salt and pepper	salt and pepper

Place the sausages in the toaster oven and grill, turning frequently, until cooked. Heat the oil in a frying pan and stir in the onion, vinegar, Worcestershire sauce, brown sugar, redcurrant jelly and all but 1 tablespoon of the tomato juice. Heat. Blend the remaining tomato juice with the cornflour and stir into the sauce. Bring to the boil and season. Spear the sausages on to cocktail sticks and dip into the sauce.

Serves 4

Illustrated on page 70

Pork stroganoff

IMPERIAL/METRIC	AMERICAN
2 oz/50 g butter	¼ cup butter
1 small onion, chopped	1 small onion, chopped
1 clove garlic, crushed	1 clove garlic, crushed
3 rashers unsmoked bacon, diced	⅓ cup diced unsmoked bacon
freshly ground black pepper	freshly ground black pepper
pinch caraway seeds	pinch caraway seeds
pinch marjoram	pinch marjoram
8 oz/225 g button mushrooms	2 cups button mushrooms
1 lb/450 g pork fillet	1 lb pork tenderloin
¼ pint/1·5 dl soured cream	⅔ cup sour cream
chopped parsley	chopped parsley

Melt the butter in an electric frying pan and sauté the onion, garlic and bacon together with the caraway seeds and marjoram, for 5 minutes. Add the mushrooms and cook for a further 5 minutes.

Slice the pork fillet and cut into thin strips. Add to the pan and cook for 10-12 minutes. Pour in the soured cream and add the chopped parsley. Serve at once with noodles. (When using an electric frying pan, the noodles can be cooked at the same time as the stroganoff. Place them in a foil dish, cover with lightly salted water and stand the dish in the pan with the stroganoff mixture around.)

Serves 4

Illustrated opposite

Tournedos in Madeira

IMPERIAL/METRIC	AMERICAN
4 tournedos steaks	4 tournedos steaks
salt and black pepper	salt and black pepper
1 oz/25 g butter	2 tablespoons butter
2 tablespoons Madeira	3 tablespoons Madeira
1 tablespoon chopped parsley	1 tablespoon chopped parsley

Season the tournedos steaks with salt and black pepper. Brown them on both sides in a hot, thick-bottomed pan. Place on a serving dish. Add the butter, allow to melt and cook for 1 minute. Pour in the Madeira and reheat. Stir in the parsley and pour over the tournedos.

Serves 4

Swiss veal

IMPERIAL/METRIC	AMERICAN
4 veal escalopes	4 veal scallops
salt and pepper	salt and pepper
4 slices ham	4 slices cooked smoked ham
4 slices Gruyère cheese	4 slices Gruyère cheese
1 egg, beaten	1 egg, beaten
fresh white breadcrumbs	fresh white bread crumbs
2 oz/50 g butter	¼ cup butter
2 tablespoons oil	3 tablespoons oil

Season the escalopes, place a slice of ham and a slice of cheese on each one. Fold each escalope over, brush with beaten egg and coat twice in breadcrumbs.

Melt the butter and oil in a frying pan and fry the escalopes gently until golden, turning once, for 10-15 minutes.

Serves 4

Peanut hamburgers

IMPERIAL/METRIC	AMERICAN
1 onion, grated	1 onion, grated
8 oz/225 g beef, minced	1 cup ground beef
pinch mixed herbs	pinch mixed herbs
salt and pepper	salt and pepper
2 tablespoons chopped peanuts	3 tablespoons chopped peanuts
1 tablespoon chopped parsley	1 tablespoon chopped parsley
1 potato, grated	1 potato, grated
few drops Tabasco sauce	few drops Tabasco sauce
1 tablespoon oil	1 tablespoon oil
4 hamburger rolls or baps	4 hamburger rolls

Combine the onion, beef, herbs, seasoning, peanuts, parsley, potato and Tabasco sauce. Divide into four and shape each into a round flat hamburger.

Heat the oil in a frying pan and cook the hamburgers on both sides until golden brown. Place each inside a roll and serve hot. If liked a few onion rings can be added to each hamburger.

Serves 4

Illustrated on page 70

Flambéed veal cutlets

IMPERIAL/METRIC	AMERICAN
2 oz/50 g butter	$\frac{1}{4}$ cup butter
4 veal cutlets	4 veal cutlets
8 oz/225 g button mushrooms	2 cups button mushrooms
1 tablespoon chopped fresh tarragon or $\frac{1}{2}$ teaspoon dried	1 tablespoon chopped fresh tarragon or $\frac{1}{2}$ teaspoon dried
2 tablespoons brandy	3 tablespoons brandy
$\frac{1}{4}$ pint/1·5 dl cream	$\frac{2}{3}$ cup cream
2 tablespoons chopped parsley	3 tablespoons chopped parsley

Melt the butter in a frying pan and brown the cutlets on both sides –
about 5-10 minutes. Add the mushrooms and tarragon and continue to
cook for 5 minutes. Pour over the warmed brandy and ignite with a
lighted match.

Place the veal on a serving dish. Reheat the juices and pour in the
cream, but *do not boil*. Add the parsley and pour the cream mixture over
the veal.

Serves 4

Chicken chop suey

IMPERIAL/METRIC	AMERICAN
1 oz/25 g butter	2 tablespoons butter
1 small onion, chopped	1 small onion, chopped
2 sticks celery, chopped	2 stalks celery, chopped
1 green pepper, chopped	1 green sweet pepper, chopped
4 oz/100 g mushrooms, sliced	1 cup sliced mushrooms
12 oz/350 g cooked chicken, cubed	$\frac{3}{4}$ lb cooked chicken, cubed
1 (9$\frac{1}{2}$-oz/269-g) can beansprouts	1 (9$\frac{1}{2}$-oz) can beansprouts
$\frac{1}{2}$ pint/3 dl chicken stock	1$\frac{1}{4}$ cups chicken stock
1 tablespoon cornflour	1 tablespoon cornstarch
2 tablespoons water	3 tablespoons water
1 tablespoon soy sauce	1 tablespoon soy sauce

Melt the butter in a frying pan and sauté the onion, celery and pepper for
2-3 minutes. Stir in the mushrooms, chicken, rinsed beansprouts and stock.
Bring to the boil and simmer for 5 minutes. Blend the cornflour with the
water and stir into the mixture, together with the soy sauce. Cook for a
further 5 minutes and serve with noodles.

Serves 4

Steak au poivre

IMPERIAL/METRIC	AMERICAN
4 teaspoons made English mustard	4 teaspoons prepared mustard
black peppercorns	black peppercorns
4 fillet steaks	4 filet steaks
salt and pepper	salt and pepper
olive oil	olive oil
butter	butter
lemon juice	lemon juice

Spread a little mustard over each steak. Crush the peppercorns with a rolling pin and press into the steaks. Season, and brush them all over with oil. Leave for 1 hour to marinate.

Heat a knob of butter in a frying pan and cook the steaks according to taste. Remove them from the pan and add a squeeze of lemon juice to the remaining butter. Pour over the steaks. Garnish with parsley, if liked, and serve with a salad.

Serves 4

Illustrated opposite

Wiener schnitzel

IMPERIAL/METRIC	AMERICAN
4 thin veal escalopes	4 thin veal scallops
seasoned flour	seasoned flour
beaten egg	beaten egg
fresh white breadcrumbs	fresh white bread crumbs
butter for frying	butter for frying
lemon juice	lemon juice
TO GARNISH:	TO GARNISH:
slices of lemon	slices of lemon
parsley	parsley

Coat the escalopes in seasoned flour. Brush with egg and roll in breadcrumbs, pressing on firmly.

Heat the butter in a frying pan and cook the escalopes for 5-10 minutes, turning them once. Place them on a serving dish and garnish with twists of lemon. Add a squeeze of lemon juice to the butter remaining in the pan and pour this over the escalopes. Garnish with parsley.

Serves 4

Boeuf stroganoff

IMPERIAL/METRIC	AMERICAN
1 lb/450 g rump steak	1 lb round steak
seasoned flour	seasoned flour
2 oz/50 g butter	¼ cup butter
1 medium-sized onion, chopped	1 medium-sized onion, chopped
4 oz/100 g button mushrooms	1 cup button mushrooms
1 tablespoon tomato purée	1 tablespoon tomato paste
½ pint/3 dl stock	1¼ cups stock
1 tablespoon brandy	1 tablespoon brandy
salt	salt
freshly ground black pepper	freshly ground black pepper
pinch nutmeg	pinch nutmeg
¼ pint/1·5 dl soured cream	⅔ cup sour cream

Cut the meat diagonally across the grain into strips 2 inches (5 cm) long and ¼ inch (0·5 cm) wide. Toss the meat in a little seasoned flour.

Heat the butter in a large frying pan and sauté the onion until softened. Add the meat and brown over a high heat. Reduce the heat and add the mushrooms, tomato purée, stock, brandy and seasoning. Just before serving, stir in the soured cream.

Serves 2-3

Saltimbocca

IMPERIAL/METRIC	AMERICAN
8 thin slices veal	8 thin slices veal
8 thin slices ham	8 thin slices smoked ham
½ teaspoon dried or 1 teaspoon chopped fresh sage	½ teaspoon dried or 1 teaspoon chopped fresh sage
1 oz/25 g butter	2 tablespoons butter
¼ pint/1·5 dl Marsala wine	⅔ cup Marsala wine
8 slices bread, toasted	8 slices bread, toasted
watercress	watercress

Using a rolling pin, beat the veal slices between dampened greaseproof paper. Place a slice of ham on top of each piece of veal and season with a pinch of sage. Roll each slice up and secure with a wooden cocktail stick.

Melt the butter and sauté the veal rolls for 5-7 minutes. Stir in the Marsala and simmer for 15 minutes.

Cut the toast into eight rounds and place a veal roll on each. Garnish with watercress and serve with fresh vegetables.

Serves 4

Chicken liver risotto

IMPERIAL/METRIC	AMERICAN
8 oz/225 g chicken livers	½ lb chicken livers
1 onion, chopped	1 onion, chopped
1 clove garlic, crushed	1 clove garlic, crushed
1 oz/25 g butter	2 tablespoons butter
4 oz/100 g mushrooms	1 cup mushrooms
8 oz/225 g long-grain rice	generous cup long-grain rice
1 tablespoon tomato purée	1 tablespoon tomato paste
1 pint/6 dl stock	2½ cups stock
salt and pepper	salt and pepper
1 (8-oz/227-g) packet frozen peas	1 (8-oz) package frozen peas

Trim the livers, removing any fat. Sauté the onion and garlic in the butter for 1-2 minutes in a flameproof dish. Stir in the livers and continue to cook until browned on the outside. Add the mushrooms, rice, tomato purée, stock and seasoning. Bring to the boil and simmer for 25-30 minutes, or until stock is absorbed, stirring occasionally. Stir in the peas 5 minutes before the end of cooking.

Serves 4

Sautéed kidneys

IMPERIAL/METRIC	AMERICAN
8 lambs' kidneys	8 lamb kidneys
seasoned flour	seasoned flour
2 oz/50 g butter	¼ cup butter
1 tablespoon brandy	1 tablespoon brandy
¼ pint/1·5 dl stock	⅔ cup stock
4 oz/100 g button mushrooms	1 cup button mushrooms
1 tablespoon tomato purée	1 tablespoon tomato paste
pinch marjoram	pinch marjoram
2 tablespoons chopped parsley	3 tablespoons chopped parsley
1 bay leaf	1 bay leaf

Remove the skin and centre core from the kidneys and toss the kidneys in seasoned flour. Heat the butter in an electric frying pan and sauté the kidneys for a few minutes. Pour over the brandy, heat for a few seconds and ignite. When the flames have died down, add the remaining ingredients. Bring to the boil and simmer for 10 minutes or until the kidneys are tender. Serve with a border of boiled rice and a mixed salad.

Serves 4

Illustrated opposite

Buttered scampi

IMPERIAL/METRIC	AMERICAN
2 oz/50 g butter	¼ cup butter
12 oz/350 g scampi	¾ lb jumbo shrimp
1 clove garlic, crushed	1 clove garlic, crushed
few drops lemon juice	few drops lemon juice
1 tablespoon chopped fresh parsley	1 tablespoon chopped fresh parsley
freshly ground black pepper	freshly ground black pepper

Melt the butter in a frying pan and gently fry the scampi for about 5-10 minutes until cooked. Stir in the crushed garlic, lemon juice, parsley and freshly ground black pepper and reheat. Serve on a bed of rice with a tossed green salad.

Serves 4

Sweet tabletop dishes

Basic pancake batter

IMPERIAL/METRIC	AMERICAN
4 oz/125 g flour	1 cup all-purpose flour
pinch salt	pinch salt
1 large egg	1 large egg
½ pint/3 dl milk	1¼ cups milk
1 oz/25 g butter	2 tablespoons butter
oil for frying	oil for frying

Sieve the flour and salt into a basin. Make a well in the centre and add the egg. Gradually add the milk, beating well until the mixture is smooth. Fold in the melted butter. Brush the base of a heavy-based 6-7-inch (15-17-cm) frying pan with oil. Allow the oil to become hot, then pour in sufficient batter to thinly cover the pan base, tilting the pan for even spreading. Cook for 1-2 minutes, then turn over to cook the other side.

Makes 6 pancakes

Blintzes

IMPERIAL/METRIC	AMERICAN
basic pancake batter (see above)	basic pancake batter (see above)
12 oz/350 g cottage cheese	1½ cups cottage cheese
2 eggs	2 eggs
¼ pint/1·5 dl single cream	⅔ cup half and half
2 tablespoons sugar	3 tablespoons sugar
pinch salt	pinch salt
1 teaspoon vanilla essence	1 teaspoon vanilla extract
1 tablespoon stoned raisins, chopped (optional)	1 tablespoon chopped pitted raisins (optional)
2 oz/50 g butter	¼ cup butter

Make the pancakes. Combine the cottage cheese, eggs, cream, sugar, salt, vanilla essence and raisins. Place a tablespoon of the filling down the centre of each pancake and roll up.

Heat the butter in a pan and gently fry the blintzes until golden. Sprinkle with sugar and serve with raspberry or strawberry jam, if liked.

Makes 8-10 blintzes

Illustrated on page 102

Crêpes Suzette

IMPERIAL/METRIC	AMERICAN
basic pancake batter (see opposite)	basic pancake batter (see opposite)
4 lumps sugar	4 lumps sugar
1 orange	1 orange
1 oz/25 g butter	2 tablespoons butter
2 tablespoons sugar	3 tablespoons sugar
1 tablespoon orange juice	1 tablespoon orange juice
1 tablespoon Curaçao	1 tablespoon Curaçao
2-3 tablespoons brandy	3-4 tablespoons brandy

Make the pancakes and keep them hot. Rub the sugar lumps over the orange skin to remove the zest. Crush the sugar lumps and mix with the butter, sugar, orange juice and Curaçao.

Place the orange butter into a heavy-based frying pan or chafing dish and allow it to melt. Fold the pancakes into four and place them, overlapped, in the pan. Baste with the butter sauce and heat through.

Pour over the brandy, allow to become warm, then ignite. When the flames have subsided, sprinkle with blanched, grated orange rind and serve immediately.

Serves 4

Illustrated on page 103

Flambéed peaches

IMPERIAL/METRIC	AMERICAN
6 ripe peaches	6 ripe peaches
$\frac{1}{2}$ pint/3 dl water	$1\frac{1}{4}$ cups water
6 oz/175 g castor sugar	$\frac{3}{4}$ cup sugar
4 tablespoons brandy	5 tablespoons brandy

Cover the peaches with boiling water for 1 minute, then plunge into cold water. Peel off the skins, halve and remove the stones.

Dissolve the water and sugar in a pan over a low heat. Pour into a chafing dish and bring to the boil and add the peaches. Poach gently for 4-5 minutes, then lift out on to a serving dish. Reduce the syrup by half, then pour over the peaches.

Warm the brandy and pour over the peaches. Ignite, then serve with cream.

Serves 6

BLINTZES (SEE RECIPE PAGE 100)

CRÊPES SUZETTE (SEE RECIPE PAGE 101)

Brandied apples in white wine

IMPERIAL/METRIC	AMERICAN
4 oz/100 g sugar	½ cup sugar
½ pint/3 dl dry white wine	1¼ cups dry white wine
½ pint/3 dl water	1¼ cups water
juice of ½ lemon	juice of ½ lemon
juice of ½ orange	juice of ½ orange
8 medium-sized dessert apples, peeled	8 medium-sized eating apples, peeled
1 oz/25 g butter	2 tablespoons butter
4 tablespoons apricot brandy	5 tablespoons apricot brandy

Dissolve the sugar in the wine and water in a saucepan. Bring to the boil and add the fruit juices. Place the peeled apples in the hot syrup and poach gently until tender, basting occasionally.

Pour the syrup into a chafing dish or heavy-based pan over a spirit burner. Place the apples carefully into the syrup. Add the butter, allow to melt and baste the apples. Warm the brandy, pour over the apples and ignite. Serve immediately with cream.

Serves 4 or 8

Illustrated on page 106

St. Clement's pancakes

IMPERIAL/METRIC	AMERICAN
basic pancake batter (see page 100)	basic pancake batter (see page 100)
1 oz/25 g butter	2 tablespoons butter
4 oz/100 g sugar	½ cup sugar
grated rind and juice of 1 orange	grated rind and juice of 1 orange
grated rind and juice of 1 lemon	grated rind and juice of 1 lemon
2 tablespoons Cointreau	3 tablespoons Cointreau

Make the pancakes. Melt the butter in a chafing dish and add the sugar, rind and juice of the fruits. Stir until the sugar has dissolved. Add the Cointreau.

Fold the pancakes into four and reheat in the sauce. Serve with cream.

Serves 4

Spiced pineapple fritters

IMPERIAL/METRIC	AMERICAN
2 oz/50 g plain flour	½ cup all-purpose flour
1 tablespoon oil	1 tablespoon oil
3-4 tablespoons water	4-5 tablespoons water
1 egg white	1 egg white
1 (1-lb 13-oz/822-g) can pineapple rings	1 (1-lb 13-oz) can pineapple rings
cooking oil for deep-frying	cooking oil for deep-frying
castor sugar to dredge	sugar to dredge
½ teaspoon mixed spice	½ teaspoon mixed spice

Combine the flour, oil and water in a mixing bowl and beat with a wooden spoon until the batter is smooth. Whisk the egg white and fold into the batter when ready to use.

Drain the pineapple well and dip the slices, one at a time, into the batter. Lower into the hot oil and cook until crisp and golden. Drain well and toss in sugar and spice, mixed. Serve with strawberry or raspberry jam.

Serves 4

Illustrated on page 107

Apricot pancakes

IMPERIAL/METRIC	AMERICAN
basic pancake batter (see page 100)	basic pancake batter (see page 100)
1 lb/0·5 kg fresh apricots	1 lb fresh apricots
½ pint/3 dl water	1¼ cups water
4 oz/100 g sugar	½ cup sugar
2 oz/50 g toasted almonds, chopped	½ cup toasted almonds, chopped
1 oz/25 g glacé cherries, chopped	1 oz candied cherries, chopped

Make the pancakes and keep them hot. Cook the apricots in the water and sugar until tender. Remove the fruit and discard the stones. Reduce the remaining syrup until thick.

Arrange the pancakes on top of each other in a flameproof dish with apricots in between. Pour over the syrup and sprinkle with toasted almonds and cherries. Serve with cream.

Serves 4

BRANDIED APPLES IN WHITE WINE (SEE RECIPE PAGE 104)

SPICED PINEAPPLE FRITTERS (SEE RECIPE PAGE 105)

Banana pancakes with butterscotch sauce

IMPERIAL/METRIC	AMERICAN
basic pancake batter (see page 100)	*basic pancake batter (see page 100)*
4 bananas, sliced	*4 bananas, sliced*
1 tablespoon lemon juice	*1 tablespoon lemon juice*
1 oz/25 g butter	*2 tablespoons butter*
1 oz/25 g soft brown sugar	*2 tablespoons light brown sugar*
SAUCE:	SAUCE:
4 oz/100 g butter	*½ cup butter*
4 oz/100 g soft brown sugar	*½ cup light brown sugar*
¼ pint/1·5 dl single cream	*⅔ cup half and half*

Make the pancakes and keep them warm. Toss the sliced bananas in the lemon juice. Melt the butter in a frying pan or chafing dish, add the bananas and brown sugar and cook gently for 3-4 minutes.

For the sauce, melt the butter and stir in the sugar. Heat until the sugar has dissolved. Cool and stir in the cream.

Divide the banana filling between the pancakes, roll them up and arrange on a serving dish. Pour over the sauce or serve separately.

Serves 4

Brandied oranges

IMPERIAL/METRIC	AMERICAN
2 oz/50 g butter	*¼ cup butter*
2 oranges, peeled and sliced	*2 oranges, peeled and sliced*
1 oz/25 g icing sugar, sieved	*¼ cup sifted confectioners' sugar*
¼ pint/1·5 dl double cream	*⅔ cup whipping cream*
1 tablespoon brandy	*1 tablespoon brandy*

Heat the butter in a chafing dish and sauté the sliced oranges for 5 minutes. Sprinkle with icing sugar. Whip the cream with the brandy and serve on top of the oranges.

Serves 2

Flambéed bananas

IMPERIAL/METRIC	AMERICAN
4 bananas	*4 bananas*
juice of ½ orange	*juice of ½ orange*
2 oz/50 g soft brown sugar	*¼ cup light brown sugar*
1 oz/25 g butter	*2 tablespoons butter*
grated rind of 1 orange	*grated rind of 1 orange*
3 tablespoons brandy	*4 tablespoons brandy*

Peel the bananas and cut in half lengthways. Place them in a buttered flameproof dish, cut side down. Sprinkle with the orange juice, sugar, dots of butter and orange rind. Cook gently for 5-10 minutes, turning frequently and basting with the juices if necessary.

Pour over the brandy and ignite. Serve at once with cream.

Serves 4

Chocolate pancakes

IMPERIAL/METRIC	AMERICAN
basic pancake batter (see page 100)	*basic pancake batter (see page 100)*
4 oz/100 g plain chocolate	*¼ lb semi-sweet chocolate*
2 tablespoons castor sugar	*3 tablespoons sugar*
¼ pint/1·5 dl water	*⅔ cup water*
1 oz/25 g butter	*2 tablespoons butter*
1 (11-oz/312-g) packet vanilla ice cream	*1 (11-oz) package vanilla ice cream*

Make the pancakes and keep them warm. Place the chocolate in a bowl over hot water, together with the sugar and water. When melted, remove from the heat and beat in the butter.

Place a spoonful of ice cream on each pancake and roll up. Pour over the chocolate sauce and serve immediately.

Serves 4

FLAMBÉED PINEAPPLE
(SEE RECIPE PAGE 112)

111

Flambéed pineapple

IMPERIAL/METRIC	AMERICAN
6 slices fresh pineapple	6 slices fresh pineapple
5 tablespoons kirsch	6 tablespoons kirsch
4 oz/100 g butter	½ cup butter
6 glacé cherries	6 candied cherries
3 tablespoons clear honey	4 tablespoons clear honey
2 tablespoons brandy	3 tablespoons brandy

Remove the peel and hard centre core from the pineapple and marinate in kirsch for 1-2 hours.

Heat the butter in a flameproof dish, add the pineapple with a cherry in the centre, kirsch and heat for 5-10 minutes. Spoon over the honey and heat for 3-4 minutes. Add the brandy and ignite. Serve with whipped cream.

Serves 6

Illustrated on pages 110-111

Brazilian pears

IMPERIAL/METRIC	AMERICAN
4 ripe pears	4 ripe pears
2 oz/50 g butter	¼ cup butter
1 oz/25 g brown sugar	2 tablespoons brown sugar
3 tablespoons brandy	4 tablespoons brandy
2 oz/50 g walnuts, chopped	½ cup chopped walnuts

Peel, core and thinly slice the pears. Melt the butter in a chafing dish and cook the pears on both sides for a few minutes. Sprinkle with sugar and pour over the brandy. Ignite with a lighted match and, when the flames have subsided, sprinkle with walnuts and serve with whipped cream.

Serves 4

Menus

Cheese and bourguignonne fondue menus

DUTCH FONDUE MENU *(for 4)*

Melon with orange slices

Dutch fondue *(see page 27)* with cubes of French bread,
celery to dip
Baked potatoes with lemon and chive butter
Mixed salad
Garlic bread

Raspberry sorbet *(see page 119)*

Serve the same wine used in the making of the fondue.

BEER FONDUE MENU *(for 4)*

Beer fondue *(see page 30)* with cubes of French bread,
previously fried in butter until golden
Tomato salad with French dressing
Green salad

Caramelised oranges *(see page 119)*

Beer

LAMB FONDUE MENU *(for 4 to 6)*

Lamb fondue *(see page 36)* with mint sauce *(see page 53)*,
orange and redcurrant sauce *(see page 61)*
and onion sauce *(see page 48)*
Swiss rosti *(see page 72)*
Sliced mushrooms tossed in French dressing

Lemon soufflé *(see page 118)*

White wine

POTATO FONDUE MENU *(for 4)*

Grilled grapefruit halves sprinkled with brown sugar

Potato fondue *(see page 38)* with
Danish blue sauce *(see page 55)* and
avocado dressing *(see page 51)*
Tossed green salad
Hot French bread

Selection of cheese and fruit

Beer

ORIENTAL FONDUE MENU *(for 6)*

Oriental fondue *(see page 37)* with sweet 'n' sour
sauce *(see page 44)*, pepper sauce *(see page 45)*,
Mexican mayonnaise *(see page 47)* and mushroom
sauce *(see page 53)*
Fried rice
Green salad

Fresh pineapple and grape salad *(see page 117)*

FONDUE BOURGUIGNONNE MENU *(for 4)*

Avocado pears with French dressing

Fondue bourguignonne *(see page 36)* with blender
barbecue sauce *(see page 46)*, peanut sauce *(see page 53)*,
orange and redcurrant sauce *(see page 61)*
and hot chilli sauce *(see page 56)*
Baked potatoes with soured cream sauce *(see page 45)*
Green salad

Chocolate brandy mousse *(see page 117)*

Red wine

Tabletop and dessert fondue menus

MENU *(for 4)*

Grapefruit and orange cocktail

Paella *(see page 82)*
Tossed green salad
French bread

Mocha fondue *(see page 67)*

White wine

MENU (for 4)

Flambéed veal cutlets *(see page 93)*
Sautéed potatoes or new potatoes
Baked tomatoes
Watercress salad

Snowflake fondue *(see page 65 – double quantity)*

White wine

MENU (for 4)

Grilled grapefruit halves with brown sugar

Chicken suprême *(see page 84)*
Fresh broccoli
Saffron rice

Cherry fondue *(see page 64)*

White wine

Desserts for menus

Fresh pineapple and grape salad

IMPERIAL/METRIC

3 oz/75 g granulated sugar
¼ pint/1·5 dl water
juice of ½ lemon
1 tablespoon kirsch
1 medium pineapple
8 oz/225 g black grapes
4 oz/100 g green grapes

AMERICAN

6 tablespoons sugar
⅔ cup water
juice of ½ lemon
1 tablespoon kirsch
1 medium pineapple
½ lb purple grapes
4 oz white grapes

Dissolve the sugar and water over a low heat. Bring to the boil and boil for 5 minutes. Allow to cool and add the lemon juice and kirsch. Peel and core the pineapple and cut into bite-size pieces. Halve and deseed the grapes. Combine the fruit with the syrup and chill. Serve with cream, if liked.

Serves 6

Chocolate brandy mousse

IMPERIAL/METRIC

8 oz/225 g plain chocolate
1 oz/25 g butter
4 egg yolks
3 tablespoons brandy
4 egg whites

AMERICAN

½ lb semi-sweet chocolate
2 tablespoons butter
4 egg yolks
4 tablespoons brandy
4 egg whites

Melt the chocolate in a bowl placed over a saucepan of hot water. (Do not overheat.) Remove from the heat and allow to cool. Beat in the butter, egg yolks and brandy.

Whisk the egg whites until fairly stiff and fold into the chocolate mixture. Place in individual dishes and allow to set for a few hours. Decorate with piped whipped cream, if liked.

Serves 6

Lemon soufflé

IMPERIAL/METRIC	AMERICAN
rind and juice of 2 lemons	rind and juice of 2 lemons
4½ oz/115 g castor sugar	good ½ cup sugar
3 large eggs	3 large eggs
½ oz/15 g gelatine	2 envelopes gelatin
4 fl oz/1·25 dl water	scant ⅔ cup water
6 fl oz/2 dl double cream	⅓ cup heavy cream

Place the lemon juice, sugar and egg yolks in a bowl and place over a saucepan of hot water. Whisk until the mixture is thick and leaves a trail. Stir in the lemon rind.

Dissolve the gelatine in the water and carefully fold into the lemon mixture. When on the point of setting, whisk the egg whites and fold into the mixture. Lightly whisk the cream and fold in. Tie a band of double greaseproof paper round a 5-6-inch (13-15-cm) soufflé dish so that it stands 3 inches (7·5 cm) above the rim of the dish. Pour the soufflé into the dish and allow to set.

Carefully remove the greaseproof paper using the back of a knife. Decorate the soufflé with piped whipped cream.

Serves 6

Caramelised oranges

IMPERIAL/METRIC	AMERICAN
6 oranges	6 oranges
3 tablespoons brandy	4 tablespoons brandy
4 oz/100 g granulated sugar	½ cup sugar
¼ pint/1·5 dl water	⅔ cup water

Carefully remove thin slices of peel, the size of a matchstick, from the oranges, sufficient to sprinkle on top of the oranges as a decoration. Cover with water, bring to the boil and drain.

Peel the oranges and remove all the pith. Cut the flesh into slices and place in a serving dish. Sprinkle with the brandy.

Heat the sugar and water until dissolved. Bring to the boil and simmer rapidly until it turns to a caramel colour. Pour over the oranges and leave for several hours or overnight to allow the caramel to form a syrup. Sprinkle with the prepared orange rind and serve with cream, if liked.

Serves 4

Raspberry sorbet

IMPERIAL/METRIC	AMERICAN
1 lb/450 g raspberries, fresh or frozen	1 lb raspberries, fresh or frozen
4 oz/100 g sugar	½ cup sugar
¼ pint/1·5 dl water	⅔ cup water
1 lemon	1 lemon
3 large egg whites	3 large egg whites

Sieve the raspberries to remove the pips. Place the sugar and water in a saucepan with the grated rind of the lemon and heat until the sugar has dissolved. Pour on to the raspberry purée. Taste and if too sweet add a few drops of lemon juice. Pour into a freezer tray and freeze either in the freezing compartment of the refrigerator or in a freezer, until just becoming thick. Remove from the freezer.

Whisk the egg whites until very stiff, then gradually whisk in the raspberry mixture. Taste again for sweetness. Return to the freezer tray and freeze until firm. Spoon into glasses and serve.

Serves 4

Drinks

Burgundy punch

IMPERIAL/METRIC

1¼ pints/7·5 dl Burgundy
2 tablespoons brandy
4-6 sugar lumps
½ cinnamon stick
juice of 2 oranges
juice of 1 lemon
1 pint/6 dl soda water or lemonade
ice cubes
slices of apple

AMERICAN

3 cups Burgundy
3 tablespoons brandy
4-6 sugar lumps
½ cinnamon stick
juice of 2 oranges
juice of 1 lemon
2½ cups soda water or Seven-Up
ice cubes
slices of apple

Place all the ingredients except the soda water or lemonade, ice cubes and apple slices in a large jug. Chill well in a refrigerator.

Just before serving, stir in the remaining ingredients and remove the cinnamon stick. Serve immediately.

Serves 6-8

Mulled claret

IMPERIAL/METRIC

2½ pints/1·25 litres claret
juice of 2 oranges
1 pint/6 dl lemonade
½ teaspoon mixed spice
4 oz/100 g soft brown sugar
2 oranges
1 lemon

AMERICAN

good 6 cups claret
juice of 2 oranges
2½ cups Seven-Up
½ teaspoon mixed spice
½ cup light brown sugar
2 oranges
1 lemon

Place all the ingredients except the oranges and lemon in a saucepan. Heat gently until the sugar has dissolved.

Slice the oranges and lemon, leaving the skin on, and float the slices on top of the mulled claret. Serve hot but *do not boil*.

Serves 6-8

Apple soda punch

IMPERIAL/METRIC

1 bottle rosé wine
¼ pint/1·5 dl apple juice
3 tablespoons brandy
1½ pints/9 dl soda water
1 lemon, sliced
1 orange, sliced
ice cubes

AMERICAN

1 bottle rosé wine
⅔ cup apple juice
4 tablespoons brandy
3¾ cups soda water
1 lemon sliced
1 orange, sliced
ice cubes

Place all the ingredients in a punch bowl, stir and serve immediately.

Serves approximately 10–12

Sangria

IMPERIAL/METRIC

1 bottle red wine
1 large bottle lemonade
1 lemon, thinly sliced
1 apple, thinly sliced
1 orange, thinly sliced
2 tablespoons castor sugar

AMERICAN

1 bottle red wine
1 large bottle Seven-Up
1 lemon, thinly sliced
1 apple, thinly sliced
1 orange, thinly sliced
3 tablespoons sugar

Chill the wine and lemonade before opening. Place the sliced fruits and sugar in a bowl and pour in the wine and lemonade. Stir and serve immediately.

Serves approximately 10

Cider cup

IMPERIAL/METRIC	AMERICAN
2½ pints/1·25 litres dry cider	good 6 cups cider
2 tablespoons brandy	3 tablespoons brandy
1½ pints/9 dl soda water	3¾ cups soda water
1 orange	1 orange
2 eating apples	2 eating apples
ice cubes	ice cubes

Place all the ingredients except the orange, apples and ice cubes in a large jug or punch bowl. Chill in the refrigerator. Just before serving, slice the unskinned oranges and apples and float on top of the cider cup with the ice cubes.

Serves 6–8

Illustrated on page 70

Spiced ginger cup

IMPERIAL/METRIC	AMERICAN
2 oz/50 g crystallised ginger, diced	¼ cup diced candied ginger
1 lemon, sliced	1 lemon, sliced
1½ pints/9 dl ginger ale	3¾ cups ginger ale
¼ pint/1·5 dl lemonade	⅔ cup Seven-Up
1 pint/6 dl water	2½ cups water
2 oz/50 g soft brown sugar	¼ cup light brown sugar
pinch nutmeg	pinch nutmeg

Place the crystallised ginger and sliced lemon in a warmed punch bowl. Place the remaining ingredients in a saucepan and heat gently until the sugar has dissolved. Pour over the ginger and lemon. Serve hot.

Serves 6

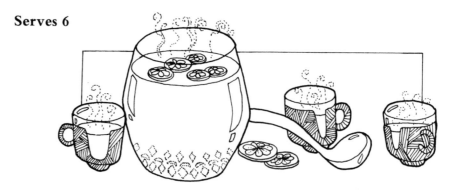

Index